AF343517

DROWNING IN ALCOHOL

Virginie Hamonnais

DROWNING IN ALCOHOL
The Story of an Alcoholic Woman

Max Milo

Max Milo, Paris, 2023
www.maxmilo.com
ISBN : 978-2-315-01139-1

To my son Thimeo,

Foreword

At thirty-five I fell into alcoholism. Two bottles of vodka a day at least and no limits: whatever else I could drink, I drank it. Alcohol, my former best friend, is the best over-the-counter anti-anxiety drug on every street corner.

I heard that for alcoholics like me, there were only four possible outcomes: prison, the psychiatric hospital, death or abstinence. I didn't go to jail, but the police station and the drunk tank did; the psychiatric hospital, I was there for a week, it was shocking; I came close to death several times. It was not easy: the madness of alcohol and death were like my shadows. The two most likely outcomes in my case. No shame and no limits... I've come a long way. A long way. Today I am totally sober.

I'm going to tell you straight about the mechanism that led me to alcoholism, the withdrawal, the cures, and everything I lost, starting with myself, and my son who was ten years old at the time. Yes, "at the time", because because of my alcoholism he was placed in 2015 in the ASE (Aide Sociale à l'Enfance) and I ruined part of his childhood and adolescence. I compromised his future when he could only count on me, as a single parent family.

I will tell you about the hell that my son and my relatives went through, the precious time that was lost forever, the loneliness, the suffering of the physical lack of the product and many other things... However, I will not tell you about the *trigger*, I never believed in it, I waited for it and it never came. Or at least not the way I thought it would, the way I expected it to.

I will talk about the difficulties to get out of it, about this daily fight to relearn how to live and regain the self-confidence that alcohol has destroyed and about the difficulty to regain the confidence of those who love you and have loved you... Because you don't want an alcoholic next to you, you avoid him, you forget him, you put him aside from your life, you make a vacuum around you. Alcohol is an expensive pit, your wallet takes a hit and your life is in danger.

I will also tell you about a taboo: it suits many people to have an alcoholic in their family, it diverts attention from the problems the family may have and fills in the gaps.

Finally, I'll tell you about the "snake" system that claims to cure you, and then releases you back into the wilderness only to return: these are the withdrawal centers and hospitals. It is a hard fight to stay sober, with people around you often in denial, the world spinning and continuing to drink, and the long follow-up you have to do to stay clean. The strength you need to stay sober. How to find the willpower and self-esteem, to be happy without alcohol, even if the problems have worsened because of alcoholism?

I gave birth to myself by getting out of this hell and writing this book... hoping that it can help alcohol addicts and their families understand and support them. Life has been the strongest, but the puzzle of myself and those around me have to be rebuilt.

Drowned in alcohol... This is my story.

CHAPTER 1
A DIFFICULT AWAKENING

One day in February 2018, I wake up and it takes me a while to figure out where I am. I have a headache. I feel numb and sluggish, I open my eyes, I'm in a hospital bed.

Unfortunately it's not the first time, I've been there so much that I know it's going to take patience, convincing to get out of there and it's going to take time. I only just woke up. I must have been in every hospital in France for the last two years so I know that once again it must have been a night that ended badly for me that got me there. I hope I didn't do too much damage the night before.

There, again, I am in a greyish white corridor of dirt in places, where people lean... A yellowish light bathes the corridor and I see squares of plasterboard on the ceiling. I am alone in this corridor, on the only stretcher. There is almost no noise, only a few beeps I hear in the distance, screams of elderly people asking for a nurse, but nothing else. They won't come. It's a waste of time.

It must be night, everything seems so quiet, you can hear a bit of the wind tunnel, it's heady, especially in my condition.

When it's night, the hospital runs slow. If you yell or scream, the nurses quickly get angry and lecture you or worse... It's best not to be noticed.

I am in a hospital, but where? Where? I only know that during this period we were with my friend, a few kilometers from Alençon in Mayenne. In the meantime I try to remember but without success, I don't remember the evening, nor how I got here.

I am covered with a white sheet up to my waist, I try to move, I can't, I can tell right away that I am strapped in my legs, I know that I don't have my shoes because my feet are cold. And my bag, where is my bag? It has all my life in it: my phone, my charger, my bank card, my cigarettes... My bag is what connects me to life, to my friend, to the outside world, it's a disaster if I don't have it with me.

I realize that my hands are also strapped on each side of my body by a thick white studded ribbon, with holes adjustable to my physiognomy so that I can't make any movement. The same goes for my chest. Impossible to get on my side or move an inch. I understood, they used the big means, I am nailed to the bed! What a shame Virginia! You've overdone it again and now you're back in the hospital, in big trouble...

I have only one idea in mind: to recover my spirits to analyze the place, to locate the exit and to smoke a cigarette. I want to go home and leave this bad dream behind me once again... I can't stand these hospital lights, these smells, these silences punctuated by a few heart beeps. It smells like death. Disinfectants and death. You hear horrible coughs, the desperate voices of old people, calling "is anyone there?" It never stops. A real horror movie. We hear furtively the voices of nurses that we do not see, but we hear them laughing from time to time, despite the repetitive and agonizing complaints that haunt these corridors...

There's no point in yelling, they won't come, the nurses. I want to tell them, but it's no use either, I repeat it in my head and wish it would stop. And at night it's a reduced team. It is better to go unnoticed and to wait, to appear normal, not to panic under the blow of impatience. Because you don't know who you are going to meet as nurses or doctors who have all the rights... They are the ones who decide: I am at their "mercy" and I am already in a bad position, strapped as I am.

I take stock. I try to move, I can't. To turn my hands to try to gain some flexibility but nothing. They really strapped me down this time! My head hurts, I reassure myself that they must have given me a shot, maybe to fill the void, to calm me down... Right now I want them to untie me, to become an ordinary patient again and go smoke. Smoking a cigarette would allow me to "breathe" a little, to get up and tame the place.

After gesticulating to evaluate the room for maneuver of all my limbs, I conclude that it is decidedly null. I am like a prisoner, punished. I come to my senses and my rather gentle and calm nature takes over... My survival instincts come back: what I want is to get out of there.

Since I woke up, I know that I am facing a test of patience: dozing while remaining vigilant in case I see a nurse, a doctor... Waiting and catching their attention at the slightest passage. My survival instinct takes over, I open my ears wide to perceive every step, in every part of the corridor to know if nurses are coming or going away. Usually they move away, and it's always a disappointment, but I have to keep my hopes up and I always do. It is easy to hear them because they all have "fangs" on their feet. At the slightest noise, I open my eyes. It makes me even more tired, I'm not quiet and I become impatient... Impossible to really rest, I want to be detached! It drives you crazy to be treated like this, to be paralyzed, to not be able to use your limbs, to be deprived of the basic freedom to come and go. I want to get out and smoke and get out of here. The time is so long. The hospital, once you go in you never know when you're going to get out. Everyone knows that, in the emergency room, it's the same thing.

I try to see the positive: except for my shoes, my coat and my bag that they kept, I am still dressed with my clothes, and not with their shirt with the naked back which makes that there, we are really completely stripped.

That's it, a sound of footsteps approaches, a nurse comes to see me. I am awake, she asks me how I am: naturally I tell her that I am very well! I ask her for a glass of water, she goes to get one and it is her who holds the glass, impossible to drink, the water runs along my chin, it drips... How can I drink in this position? I can't even lift my head. I ask her to untie me to drink and I explain to her that my wrist hurts so much they tightened it. She tells me that she has no right, and that since I am awake, a doctor will come to see me.

She leaves, so I have to wait again... Waiting and waiting again, trying to wriggle to gain a little flexibility in the links. It's stronger than me, I have to move, I try. It is lost but I try. It is my living body which also tries to take over. That's why my wrist hurts, nothing to do, and yet I put all my strength into it.

No clock. Time seems endless. I close my eyes and I wait... Always this smell of hospital... I turn my head towards the wall to forget where I am for a few moments.

I don't know how long it took for the doctor, a woman, to finally come and see me. She asks me how I am, I tell her that I am much better, that, yes, I have abused alcohol, but that I cannot stay there because I have to start a new job later (I am lying, I show the urgency that I have to leave the hospital). We are late at night. I tell myself that she will understand that I want to get ready for my job. I quickly explain to her that I am on RSA, that I need to work. There is no emergency, it is the night but she is in a hurry. While talking to me, she checks my straps and she notices that everything is indeed too tight. She notices that I am calm, that I express myself well. I finally feel a sense of understanding, so I insist, I would like to know when I can get out of the hospital, there I feel her less willing, she answers me quickly: "I'll see, I come back, I call a nurse for the straps." When the doctor is there, you should never miss the opportunity because once gone, you have to wait a long time to see one again and it is always short. She leaves, she is not talkative, she must see people like me often... But she already gives her agreement for the straps to be removed and goes to see a colleague to see if I can leave and go home.

Chapter 2
The good life and Corsica

In June 1999, I had just finished my second year of law school at the University of Paris-Nanterre, but it didn't suit me. I didn't see myself in the careers offered by these studies, I didn't want to be a lawyer, judge or bailiff. In fact, I was looking for myself.

I was doing small jobs for an agency as a hostess in trade shows, receptions for big companies, committees. I was poorly paid but at least I was working and I liked to discover these different environments, to see how these businessmen and women behaved between two conferences. Listening to their discussions, I understood that I didn't want to be part of the "corporate" world either, to feel trapped in a system.

I wanted to be free like my parents in a way. My father and mother always worked together, running a small interior design store in the 15th arrondissement of Paris. Even if there were constraints, they were creative and independent. They were the ones who managed their time and this allowed my mother to take care of me and my brother, perhaps a little more than if she had worked

19

in a "real" business. But I couldn't see myself taking over their store. My father had attended the Ecole Boulle and started working at fourteen. He worked with wood, leather and fabrics. It's a job of passion where you don't count your hours when you aim for perfection. He would go to clients' homes to take measurements, bring them the chairs, and imagine interior plans for these apartments. My mother, on the other hand, mainly received clients, advising them on the choice of fabrics. I also liked to see her busy rearranging the two windows that faced the street. They never stood idly by waiting for the customer. They were both extremely complementary and courageous.

They taught me that you don't get something for nothing, that you have to be brave, that anything is possible. They gave me a good basis to grow and evolve by myself. To believe in myself.

When summer came, they closed for two months and we spent the vacations between the country house, located in the Nièvre, and Corsica. So in 1999, the summer of my 20th birthday, I went, as every year, to South Corsica in Santa-Guillia with my family.

We would leave in the early morning to take the boat that led to Corsica, in Marseille or Toulon, on which we traveled at night. We saw the continent going away on the bridge, then we went to the restaurant, before joining our small cabin in which we heard the noise of the engines. We got up early in the morning to admire the Corsican coasts which approached. When we got off the boat with the car, with the windows open, we could smell the sweet smell of the maquis.

My parents rented a small apartment near the beach for three weeks. As soon as we took our stuff out of the car, we left to see the sea. The next morning, I let my parents and my brother get ready and have their breakfast while I was already ready to run to the beach. I liked going alone. I liked those morning smells, that there was hardly anyone on the beach yet. I felt alive: Corsica was our corner of paradise that I had known since my childhood.

That year, something happened that would change my summer. I was gently hit on by a group of young boys. We met without difficulty on the beach to talk and laugh about everything and anything. The boys were spotted by a team of M6 who wanted to follow young vacationers for *Zone Interdite.* I refused to be filmed but I got along with the film crew which was composed of a journalist, a cameraman and the sound engineer. So I followed them everywhere or almost everywhere but off camera. They talked to me about their work and the different reports they had already done, the places they had been, the people they had met. I was fascinated by what they did. A job where the objective was to tell stories! Never before would I have dared to believe that such a job could exist. I observed how the shooting went: the different sequences with the boys, the pictures of the beach, of Corsica... At each break, they became the kings of the beach, of the bars, of the discotheques... Everyone knew them. The freedom of their profession was there: wherever they went, they shot and then they put the camera down and drank a beer or two...

Even though they drank quite a bit, they were still professionals. As for me, I drank too, but much less. I drank mainly in the evening. I couldn't keep up during the day, with the sun it would have been unbearable. I didn't feel like it either, what I was experiencing gave me so much adrenaline!

One of the sequences of the documentary took place in the fashionable nightclub, Via Notte. You could see the boys dancing and partying. Flirting and being flirted with. The atmosphere was in full swing... Soon we were all heading for the bar, and everyone was drinking and dancing with a glass in hand. One whiskey and coke, then two, then three, I was drunk, but nice. I was a happy drunk in those days. I knew when to stop. That was the most important thing. I had a notion of the last drink.

The cameraman, Julio, was Corsican, from a well-known family on the island, and the son of the producer of the story. He was a proud boy, sure of his Corsican-Colombian charm and aura, but also of what he had accomplished in his life as a journalist. He took the time to explain the circumstances of the conflicts he had covered in different countries like Iraq or Liberia. He would talk about how he went about getting accepted and making contacts with people from all walks of life in the opposing camps... He was not afraid to take risks and that made him proud: you can only be impressed when you hear all those stories. We had a great complicity. He was always kicking me under the table. I had no idea at the time that Julio would, many years later, become the father of my son. It was completely improbable because he was in a relationship. He had a partner, Michelle, who was pregnant. They were expecting a baby girl in January. Julio was proud to show the picture of his "wife" who looked very pretty, but he was still charming with me. I thought it was in his nature to play. I kept my distance from him.

One day, for a sequence on a boat with the young people, I found myself with Julio who was filming and me who had to hold the sound engineer's boom. So I was behind the camera with professional equipment in my hands, having to be careful that the boom was not in the cameraman's frame while the boat was going fast and moving a lot...

The shooting finished, the team and Julio went back to Paris. My vacation ended more calmly, with my family, and with the desire to be a journalist in the back of my mind. I finally knew what I wanted to do with my life.

Chapter 3
The birth of a vocation

Back in Paris, Julio, the sound engineer and I got back in touch. We used to meet from time to time at the end of the day near Bastille. Journalist friends would join us and each of us would talk about our experiences around the world. We had a favorite bar, Le Select. We had become a band of friends... Every evening was an excuse to meet up and talk, laugh and drink. I also drank, not at the same rate but I got used to it. I was brought up as a well-behaved little girl, in a rather protected environment with my parents. When I was around them, I would let loose a little and drink more. They seemed to have no limits.

Little by little, they introduced me to several other journalists and Julio proposed that I come to the production to see how the editing was going. This was not a problem since the production was his father's. I was starting to be part of this world, at first without any real legitimacy, but I was so interested that I went ahead and finally dared to ask journalists if I could attend some of the shoots. They agreed and I went to the ones in Paris where I knew I wouldn't be a burden. I was carrying the camera stand, the bags of tapes... I was particularly following a woman journalist, Sylvie. I was in admiration of this independent journalist. I watched how she worked with the witnesses, how she managed her team. I realized how complete this job was, between the investigations, the research, the travels in different universes, the editing that finalized the work, the writing of the comments and the judicious advices of the editors who supervised the whole.

The contact was as good with the journalists, the team members as with the witnesses. The more I attended, the more I confirmed that I was made for this job. I was at a "good school" because I realized that the production from which Julio came was one of the best in Paris and in France.

For his part, Julio had become the father of a little Melissa in January 2000. He seemed happy even though I knew that there were ups and downs in the couple he formed with Michelle, with sometimes strong arguments, but I didn't interfere. I had only met Michelle once or twice. She was rather reserved and distant. She had a "cold" beauty. I thought that Julio's and Michelle's characters were really different and that maybe that's why he came home late when he was in Paris, preferring to stay at the Select with us.

At that time I saw my school friends much more than Julio and his friends but we still kept in touch when they were not away on a shoot. Then came the summer of 2002 and my first job at Réservoir Prod, Jean-Luc Delarue's production company... It was summer in Paris and they were short of staff for the interviewers and to prepare for the new school year. I introduced myself, I got my internship agreement with my first letter of recommendation from Julio's production and I could finally start working, for real.

For my first mission, I was asked to investigate alcoholism, the theme being: "Leave everything for Love". The theme was: "Quit everything for love". I had to find a young man, a young father who loved his wife and children enough to quit drinking... If I had known what was waiting for me...

From call to call, my investigation progressed and I found myself in contact with La Croix bleue, an association to fight against alcoholism, whose president herself had suffered for years. Her son also suffered from it. With the agreement of my editor-in-chief, I went to Calvados to meet this woman and another family, with my little camera, my notebook and my pen, my first production unit, my first hotel room reserved by the production company. I was happy as anything.

The president of the association accompanied me to meet the other family. We arrived in a street where all the houses looked alike and where the poverty was obvious. I quickly realized that they were so afraid to meet a "journalist" from Paris (I was 23 years old at the time) that they had been drinking before seeing me... It was incredible. I couldn't believe it. The room smelled of alcohol, the glasses were on the table and the family members were red with alcohol, they could hardly speak normally and kept interrupting each other, it was not easy for my interview.

Their story was terrible because they were all in it, the parents, the son, the brother, even to the point of dipping into each other's wallets to get alcohol. They told me that as soon as a bottle, of any kind of alcohol, was opened, they finished it during the day and that it was not enough, they always needed another one. They couldn't live without it. I was immersed in their addiction, and I was shocked. I had never seen this before, I didn't know it could be this bad. Only the young woman didn't drink and she couldn't take it anymore. She was threatening to take the kids and leave.

And I understood her.

They were all part of the association but nothing changed for them. The awareness was there but the need for alcohol was stronger, even with the children who were young.

It was the region of the coffee-calva in the morning. The president of the association herself had kept a barrel of gnole in her cellar for years. A former alcoholic, she had almost killed her son with a shotgun one night when she had drunk too much... She had decided to react, to seek treatment and to help other alcoholics in order to help herself. What I didn't understand was that before leaving she offered to take a bottle with me, which I refused. When you know what poison it is, you don't offer it.

I came back from these meetings shaken, not having once in mind that it could happen to me one day, that I could also fall so low. I was very far from thinking that alcohol would take a very important place in my life...

I learned a few years later that the son of the president of the Blue Cross had committed suicide after drinking too much. This woman was devastated, but what can I say? I could hear in her voice that she had relapsed.

The next day, I went back to Reservoir with my images, I was right on topic but the family was not "good" enough to be on TV.

They were too into alcohol, and not proper enough (the young father was missing teeth). It was too pathetic.

I was happy to return to my Parisian offices and I knew that I had found my way... I was anchored in my time, witnessing my contemporaries, the society in which I lived. The world belonged to me, everything was possible. I thought that this work could only enrich me personally, but one cannot escape unscathed from the misery of others. I will always remember their stories, each one more dramatic than the next. How could I know that one day I would give up everything and destroy myself and my family? It was inconceivable and so far from me.

In 2003 I continued my studies and I had to do another internship during the school year. I heard from a technician that they were looking for someone to work at RTL. He gave me the contact information, which I did and it worked out. I was in charge of writing the questionnaires and testing the future candidates of the program "Le Quitte ou Double", presented by Jean-Pierre Foucault.

I kept in touch with Julio who had separated from Michelle with whom things were not going well. He went to live for a while with a friend not far from the Select and we got closer. Naturally we became lovers. We went for walks with his daughter Melissa in the Montsouris park, which was next to his old apartment. He seemed to be a good father, attentive and loving. We would walk, she would run in the alleys of the park, we would sit down to eat an ice cream... We lived in the moment and these moments gave me confidence in the future.

When we were making love, Julio kept saying to me while holding my hair in a sexy and wild way "you are mine, tell me you are mine". And I would tell him. And then he kept telling me "I'm having a baby with you, I want a baby with you". Our relationship had become very strong. We were inseparable. Julio came to live in my little studio in the 15th.

At the same time, he was beginning to specialize as a war reporter. This did not reassure me, but he was passionate about the conflicts that were taking place in the world since September 11. He secretly dreamed of obtaining the Albert Londres prize, the highest award for a war reporter.

In December 2003, Julio had a solo project of reporting in Indian Kashmir on the Indo-Pakistani border. He proposed me to accompany him. So we left together with a simple tourist visa on December 25, 2003. We spent two weeks meeting the victims of attacks that took place almost daily. I will always remember the women's cries in the form of songs filled with suffering.

Julio was filming and reporting, I was accompanying him but for security reasons, I stayed with the fixer who was part of the AFP and who accompanied us everywhere. It was difficult and exciting at the same time. I discovered what Julio was going through when he went to these countries and I discovered his way of working on the spot, of gathering information and taking notes in his notebook, of filming the survivors during the attacks, of recovering the pieces of flesh of the victims which were scattered everywhere. I also had a small camera, I filmed everything and I was surprised to see that despite the horror of the scene, the fact of having the lens in front of me put a certain distance with what was happening.

The days were trying. That brought us much closer with Julio because we lived each moment with passion. We felt like privileged witnesses of what was happening there and as we were staying on a houseboat, we came back every evening with a small motorboat that was waiting for us on the shore and came to pick us up early in the morning with the mist on the lake.

The scenery was beautiful with the Himalayan mountains in the distance and when night fell we listened to The Beatles, especially the song *Across the Universe* with Ravi Shankar.

Once the report finished, we went to spend a few days in Kerala, in Trivandrum in a magnificent hotel. There it was South India with all its colors and perfumes. Julio made me crazy about him, he was full of attentions for me, took me to beautiful places, very privileged.

Then we left for France. After this month together we had become really inseparable. I was proud of him, admiring his coolness and his abilities. He told me that he loved me, that I was beautiful and sexy... He treated me like a queen. This only fueled my taste for adventure and I loved it with him, even though I couldn't see myself doing exactly the same job, with so many risks. And what was supposed to happen happened... By dint of making love and saying to myself over and over again "I want to have your child", I ended up pregnant. I told him the news, after a test and a blood test, when he returned from a trip to the Ivory Coast.

We were both the happiest people in the world. He hoped it would be a son. He had me do a test with a knife and a spoon, each covered with a cushion, to try to guess the sex of our child. I sat on the cushion that covered the knife. He was now certain it would be a boy, he said it worked every time. He seemed to be really happy and proud. My parents

Chapter 3 The birth of a vocation

were happy when they heard I was pregnant, but a little wary because they didn't think Julio was very stable. Fortunately, I have always been close to my parents and I knew I could count on them. What I didn't know yet was how important their presence would be by my side.

CHAPTER 4
MY SON, MY GREATEST HAPPINESS
AND THE LIES

The year 2004 was the year of my pregnancy. We left the small studio to go, still in the 15th district, in a two-room apartment that my mother lent us. This apartment had a history, it was the one in which she had grown up with my grandmother.

It was located on rue Lecourbe at the corner of rue Cambronne, just above a bar, Les Artisans. As we passed in front of it several times a day, we quickly got to know the waiters and the owner who was kind. He knew my parents and was kind to us. It must be said that we were good customers! We often had lunch there with my parents or Julio and quickly *Les Artisans* became his HQ. He would meet his friends there to talk about his projects.

Julio was a restless man: as soon as he came back from a report, he was already thinking about the next one. So he was not often there, and when he was, he spent a lot of time in the bar to see his friends and prepare his investigations... He was going to leave several times to Guatemala, Kosovo, Congo...

I went alone to my doctor's appointments, to the obstetrician, to find the maternity ward where I was going to give birth. Between two shootings, Julio was still able to attend the second ultrasound. I was happy that he was there... The consultation went very well and we were able to see our baby's little head and nose in profile. That's when we learned that our child was going to be a boy.

Julio was proud and happy. It was a pleasure to see. I was happy to be able to share this important moment with him. The name was already chosen: Thimeo. I didn't really have a choice because the family tradition was to give the name of the paternal grandfather or the great-grandfather. I didn't mind because I liked the name and I was sure that it would suit our son.

On the night of the ultrasound, Julio introduced me to a friend of his, Camilla, a Corsican lawyer who was older than him and who seemed quite friendly. She was his old neighbor, as she lived on the floor above Michelle, Melissa's mother. We started calling each other, she would reassure me when I didn't understand Julio's absences and tell me that he was really in love, faithful and happy to be the future father of our child. I needed to hear those words, that someone was witnessing that Julio really loved me and that our child was a totally wanted child.

Julio confided in her a lot... and for good reason! Later, I would learn that they had been lovers, and that Julio had introduced me to his mistress. He also played with her because, at the time, when he was arguing with Michelle, Julio only had to go up one floor to spend the night with Camilla. But this Camilla did not admit to me until much later. I had no idea the night we had dinner together.

Julio's behavior started to change without me really noticing. When he was in Paris, he spent a lot of time outside. I had him on the phone but he would tell me whatever he wanted. He would come home late, sometimes very late, and always drunk, which led to arguments. He would have jealousy fits for no reason since I didn't see anyone, except for a few girlfriends but very rarely.

My pregnancy was actually lived with my parents, especially with my mother who was not far away. I would go to visit her and talk to her about what I knew about Julio, about the steps I was taking for the baby, about my days... And about myself of course. I would tell her that I was lonely and she understood that very well.

I wasn't working. I hadn't finished my last year of journalism school and had only done two internships. And I wasn't going to look for a job when I was pregnant. I was preparing the arrival of the baby, his things... I wanted the baby to have the coziest, happiest and softest bed possible.

I was also walking around a lot and I remember that I stopped in front of the church in Vaugirard to pray that my pregnancy would go well, that I, that we, would have a baby in good shape and without health problems. That we would be a happy and united family. I'm not religious, but in difficult times, the church is a good refuge to confide in, talk to oneself and keep confidence.

I prayed very hard and cried a lot. I couldn't understand the behavior of the man who said he loved me, I was afraid for him because of his shootings and I felt too alone. But I was focused on my pregnancy and I still wanted to trust Julio, I didn't take the time to face the truth.

I would talk to the child I was carrying, tell her it was going to be okay. That I would try to give him the best life I could. That he would be a happy boy and that I would always look out for him.

I lived with the rhythm of Julio's phone calls, which didn't last long but were always enough to make me anxious about what might happen to him. One day when I was feeling so abandoned and tired of living my pregnancy alone, I went to the Bon Marché, the Parisian department store, on the verge of despair, with the intention of buying myself a beautiful teddy bear. I went straight to the toy department in the basement and picked up the softest, cutest teddy bear I could find: a real brown teddy bear with a soft look that I could hold. It was like a feeling, a transference of love, the instinctive need for a concrete presence, that I could hug in the apartment, in my bed. Yes, the need for a presence.

Then one evening while I was taking my bath alone at home, I felt a little kick that made me jump... Finally! My baby was moving, it was wonderful! I became aware that he was really there, his presence was becoming more and more concrete.

After an X-ray, the doctor told me that I would be having a C-section because my pelvis was too narrow for a normal procedure, so I had to set a delivery date. He suggested January 13, which I refused because Julio's daughter Melissa was born on January 12 and I didn't want our son's birthday to come after his. I had a bad feeling about what was going on with Julio, I felt that he was hiding something from me but I didn't know what. So I asked my doctor to let me know if there was room before January 12. I explained to him why it was so important to me and he understood.

I had taken every step alone, I had to make this decision alone. This question of the day of birth was a way to affirm myself and our child, our relationship. Suddenly I was no longer passive, I was making a meaningful decision that I thought was best for my son.

Julio didn't know the date of the birth because he had to leave for Indonesia after the tsunami of January 4, 2005 to be one of the first journalists on the spot. With what had happened there, there was no way to reach him by phone, and somehow I thought that it was a good thing, I had lived my pregnancy alone, I felt ready to give birth alone. The doctor called me on Friday, January 7 and told me that the delivery would take place early: Tuesday, January 11, 2005. What a relief! It was so important to me! My wish was granted.

My parents accompanied me to the clinic on Monday evening with my bags and the clothes for the baby that I had carefully prepared. I was serene and surrounded by my family, their love. I still left a voice mail message on Julio's answering machine telling him that I was due the next morning at nine o'clock. I had my teddy bear in the room like a good luck charm. The midwives were warm, I was looking forward to meeting my little guy and holding him in my arms. I fell asleep serenely.

On January 11, 2005, at 8:30 a.m., while I was on the operating table and had just received the epidural, who do I see coming? Julio! He explained that he had received my message when he got off the plane and that he had rushed to the clinic. He had time to kiss me on the mouth and was asked to go to a room next door, as the moment had arrived: Thimeo was about to be born.

They put a cloth over me so I couldn't see anything, I was a little woozy, but I could hear everything that was going on and after a few short minutes, the doctor put my son on top of me. He was beautiful! Just born, he was already smiling, I could feel his warmth, his breath... he was already the most beautiful baby in the world! My baby was fine, he was perfect and finally here.

Julio was called by the doctor to give Thimeo the first care and the first hug. I then went to the resting room, Thimeo in his incubator next to me. I was serene, happy and amazed... tired but amazed. Thimeo was there. I did not leave him of the eyes. My parents were there too and I had a visit from Julio's father, Carlos, who came to see his grandson. I was tired and not quite awake, the visit was brief but I was rather reassured because as Julio had told me, family for Corsicans is the most important thing. He finished the day with his friends drinking at the local café to celebrate the birth of his son.

I went back to the room with my baby, every move felt so natural. I had waited and wanted my son so much! That's when I put the teddy bear in Thimeo's bed, the teddy bear and all the hopes I had put in it were now his...

Thimeo was born on January 11, 2005, he was recognized by his father on January 13 at the town hall of the 15th. Julio must have spent January 12 with his daughter since it was her birthday, I didn't see him that day but it didn't surprise me. I was with my son, pampering him between two visits, I didn't think about it. January 14 was the day I was to have my staples removed.

The nurse came into my room and began her work. It hurt like hell, but I had no idea what would happen a few minutes later, when someone knocked on the bedroom door. It was Julio's ex-girlfriend, Michelle, Melissa's mother. The nurse interrupted her work and left me alone with her and my baby in the room. I didn't understand why she was there, in the safe space that was my room with Thimeo... Even lying on the bed, not being able to move, I was on guard, I didn't want her to get close to Thimeo.

And then, Michelle, straight as an I, turns into a real fury in an instant, telling me that Julio and her had never really ended even if they had taken a "break" in their story. She told me that she had gone to Indonesia with him, that they had met again and that it was her that Julio loved...

She tells me that they got my message about the birth just off the plane, together in the cab, and that before coming to the clinic, he had dropped her off at her house, that he had even given her an engagement ring during the trip to Indonesia. She shows me the ring on her finger, and above all she yells at me saying that Julio would never recognize our son. That Julio had never loved me.

In my head, I was thinking at that moment that it was too late, that Julio had recognized Thimeo at the town hall the day before. I didn't say anything so as not to increase her anger, I let her talk and congratulated myself for having brought forward the date of the birth.

Michelle was so angry that I didn't want it to overwhelm me and stay too long. Thimeo was there, he had not heard her insults and her voice full of hatred towards us.

The nurse came back to finish her work and asked me if everything was okay. I was shocked and couldn't understand what had happened. I looked at my son in his incubator with

Chapter 4 My son, my greatest happiness and the lies

tears in my eyes and said to him in my heart, "Don't worry my love, it's going to be okay." I waited until the nurse left to call Julio and tell him what had just happened. He told me not to worry and didn't give me any more explanations, except that Michelle was a little crazy and that he would check on me later.

He arrived in the evening with a bouquet of flowers and told me that the reason he had left with Michelle was to make her accept the situation. I was so stunned by this day and Michelle's arrival that I half listened to his explanations. I was even anxious for him to leave and take these negative waves with him, away from my son and me. I didn't want to hear anything but he left like the charmer he was, trying to reassure me and telling me he would come back the next day, which he did.

I didn't see, or didn't want to see, things coming for Julio. All my worries during my pregnancy turned out to be true, so my uncertainties did make sense, he had not been faithful to me at that time. I tried to forgive him, Julio played a lot on the fact that he was in a dangerous job, that he might die, that we were important to him. That I and Thimeo were his new family...

CHAPTER 5
SEPARATION RATHER THAN SUFFERING

When I left the clinic, I wanted to forget what had happened and focus on our future and try to believe again... but the first night we went to a restaurant with Julio's friends and when I came back he continued the evening with them... When I didn't hear from Michelle anymore, I thought she had finally left us alone. In reality Julio saw her every day because she was editing the report on the tsunami. When I found out, he explained that she needed to work and that he couldn't let her down because she was the mother of his daughter.

The happiness of being reunited all three was therefore short-lived. Soon Julio resumed his habits at the bar with his friends. I put up with it because I loved taking care of my son. I was amazed to see him grow up, to hear him laugh. Since Thimeo was here I didn't feel so alone anymore... The downside was in the evening, when I was waiting for Julio to have dinner and he didn't come... And when he did come, he was never sober. In the best of cases, he was smiling and fell asleep very quickly, but sometimes he was also a bad drunk.

When he said he was having a hard day, I knew I had to keep my mouth shut to avoid an argument; of course I couldn't always do that, so I would raise my voice and ask him how I could trust him with everything he had put me through, everything that had happened.

February 10, 2005 was my birthday, I was looking forward to Julio on my 26th birthday, my first birthday as a mother... It was important to me...

Julio didn't come home too late, but he arrived mad. He had been drinking and had a jealousy fit because the owner of the bar downstairs, knowing that it was my birthday, had left a bottle of champagne in front of the apartment door. He started to say that there was something between us, which was more than ridiculous: if Julio spent his nights at the Artisans, I just greeted the owner when I saw him. Julio wouldn't listen. He pushed me against the glass door that led to the living room. I fell and the glass broke. I was lucky to be okay. Thimeo, who was sleeping in the bedroom, woke up and started crying. I was crying too. I didn't want to scream and scare my son, so I calmly asked Julio to leave the apartment. I couldn't take it anymore. I was distraught, tired of this life that was so far from the one I had imagined. Julio went down to the bar and the next day, as usual, he acted as if nothing had happened, he even told me that he loved me and I played along.

Very quickly, Julio had to go back to shooting - I think it was in Iraq this time. Like every time he left, I burst into tears, afraid that he would not come back. Julio was crying too, he took Thimeo in his arms and told him he loved him, then he left. The apartment seemed empty and I was afraid for him, but I also felt that I could resume my role as a mom without worrying. When he was away, the house was quiet, there was no longer the stress of knowing when and in what state Julio would return. We found a certain serenity with Thimeo. Life was peaceful...

The worst thing is that when Julio was to come back, I was anxious. I knew that the peace and quiet I had experienced in his absence would not last. Of course he was happy to see us again, but he would rush out of the house. He always had something to do. I didn't understand what he was doing, so I regularly phoned Camilla, the lawyer friend that Julio had introduced to me. We would try to figure out his schedule together since she was always in touch with him. I think he even went to sleep at her house several times, because he sometimes slept over.

It went on like that for a year, with departures and returns, calm and stress, reunions and solitude... Nothing changed.

In January 2006, after returning from the shoot and by mutual agreement, Julio did not come home. We had argued on the phone and I didn't want him to come back. He answered me that it was also convenient for him. Even though I knew it was the best decision, it was still a shock. How I cried!

However, it was out of the question that we continue to live in these conditions. I was not respected and loved as I wanted to be, neither as a woman nor as a mother. Julio didn't pay enough attention to his son. He would hug him on rare occasions and tell him that he loved him, but love is not just something to be said, it has to be shown, lived and shared. It's too easy to say "I love you" and walk away. I didn't want to live in constant anxiety anymore and have my son feel it.

Thimeo was one year old.

CHAPTER 6
MY PROFESSIONAL BEGINNINGS
AND THE INSTABILITY OF THE FATHER

In 2006, I was able to find a place in a crèche in Thimeo. I needed to work again, for my personal development and because I was almost penniless; it was my parents who helped me financially. Armed with my two internships and letters of recommendation from Réservoir Prod and RTL, I showered the production companies with my CVs, but I only got negative responses...

I wanted to find a job on my own, without going through Julio or his family, so when I heard that the first TV show in Paris was going to be held at the Porte de Versailles, with all the presenters of the moment, I went for it!

There I lined up to meet Karine Lemarchand, who was presenting "Les maternelles", she immediately listened to me and asked if I was available during the summer vacations. She took my CV and told me that she was going to pass it on to her editor-in-chief. I was happy, it was my only touch but I felt good about it.

The following week, I received this famous phone call, and I managed to get an appointment in Boulogne. Karine Lemarchand was going to have a new show, "Les Tabous" for France 2, and I was going to be in charge of the casting with other journalists. That was it, my career was really starting, and I was all the more proud of it because I owed it only to myself!

I would start the following Monday, my son would be in daycare and my mom would pick him up until I got home.

I was able to choose the themes on which I was going to work and I was told that I would be the only one responsible for the set and for all the witnesses on a subject determined in advance. I chose themes that did not seem obvious to me to prove that I was competent and that I could be counted on: death (loss of a child, euthanasia), prostitution, racism, homosexuality...

Julio would call to check up on me and come back from time to time, without warning. He would knock on the door but he was often drunk and I wouldn't open it for him. When I let him in, he said he had a hard time leaving us. Sometimes he would stay for dinner and we would have sex. I was always in his grip. It went on for a while like that.

One day, when Julio came back from a shoot, he called me to tell me that he was hospitalized for a respiratory problem but that he was not contagious. He wanted us to come to Percy to see him and Thimeo, whom he hadn't seen in a long time. When we arrived, his buddies had just passed and he had a bottle of whiskey hidden in his sheets. He bragged about it as soon as we got back to his room. I sensed that it was going to get bad again. He was sick, drunk, and the first

Drowning in alcohol

thing he said to me, in a humorous tone, was, "Hi Honey, you're lucky I don't have AIDS!"

Afterwards, Julio changed addresses as much as his girlfriends. We didn't keep in touch much, but from time to time he asked to see his son. So I tried to organize meetings in the square, I didn't want to leave Thimeo alone with an alcoholic father, even if it seemed important to me to maintain a link.

I can't count the times he cancelled his appointments at the last minute because he was too drunk or didn't show up at all and didn't answer the phone, leaving us waiting and disappointed.

Sometimes he would come to have a taste with Melissa. I would see him arrive on his scooter when he was drunk. I didn't say anything because I didn't want to cause a fuss, but I thought Michelle was not aware that she was entrusting her daughter to him. As I wanted the children to have a good time, I took them to the Saint-Lambert square where there was a sandbox, a merry-go-round... while Julio stayed at home, on the sofa.

When I look at the pictures I took at the square I see Melissa has a sad and thoughtful look on her face on the carousel... She was seven years old, she was very happy to be with her little brother but she certainly expected to spend these good moments with her father too... Thimeo, on the other hand, didn't realize all these things yet.

After working six months on the show "Tabous" with Karine, I did a series of missions for France2, E=M6... As an intermittent of the spectacle, I alternated periods where I did not work and where I could take care of Thimeo every day

Chapter 6 My professional beginnings and the instability of the father after the school and periods where I worked a lot and where my mother took the relay at the house.

In 2008, as I was good at using a camera and my interviews were good, I went from being a camera operator to a JRI (Journalist Image Reporter) and I was hired on the show "Tellement vrai" for NRJ12. I also worked as a cameraman for Endemol on the show "Bienvenue chez les Sander". I loved the work of the image, using the camera to highlight the people whose testimony I collected.

I spent all my free days taking care of Thimeo, we did a lot of things together and I wanted to enroll him in the library. So I went to the library of the 15th district to borrow beautiful books for children. At the time of registering my son, I was asked to show the family record book! Indeed Thimeo does not have my name and I had to prove that I was his mother! We left disappointed and angry.

This episode made me think and I thought that since I had no more news from Julio, it could cause a lot of problems if my son didn't have both our family names. As I couldn't see myself carrying the family book for every formality, I phoned Julio to explain the problem and ask him to come with me to the town hall so that we could do the necessary steps.

After many unanswered phone calls, discussions that he ended by hanging up on me, and appointments at city hall that he didn't show up for, he finally told me he wouldn't do it and that my last name was ugly anyway!

I was in a rage: he had not only insulted me, he had insulted my family. Moreover, while he had become almost non-existent in his son's life, he was clearly preventing me from exercising my rights as a mother and being recognized as such.

And then I started to think that it would be normal for him to pay alimony to participate in the "maintenance" of his son. In short, I simply wanted Julio to finally assume his responsibilities and that the Justice system put some order in his relationship with me but especially with his son, so that things would be clear. I thus undertook a first step with the TGI of Paris, with the JAF (the judge with the family business) so that is fixed the principal residence of Thimeo at my place and that the father has a maintenance allowance to pay.

On July 13, 2009, a first decision was rendered by the Paris Court of First Instance, which states that: parental authority will be exercised jointly; the child's habitual residence will be fixed at his mother's; the father will have the right to see his son according to his schedule and availability on certain weekends and during school vacations for a period of five days; and orders Julio to pay a maintenance allowance of 200 euros per month for the upkeep and education of his child.

Obviously the procedure did not stop there, I had to write to the clerk of the court to get what is called "a certificate of non-appeal of the decision", necessary to contact a bailiff and to enforce the judgment with the father.

I might as well say right away that he never paid any alimony, even those 200 euros that meant nothing to him or his family. The bailiffs could not do anything because he did not take the registered letters with acknowledgment of receipt, and when they went to the place he never opened the door. However, the bailiffs' investigations of the neighbors said that he lived at this address. So this decision did not help much...

But there was no question of depriving ourselves for all that! I did not want Thimeo to suffer from these difficulties and in August 2009, we left for his first big trip, ten days in the Dominican Republic in the south of the island, on the Caribbean side.

We swam, visited the neighboring villages in *guaguas*, the local buses... It was a real vacation, far from the worries. He was small but I wanted him to discover wonders, the world, different languages...

Then the daily life resumed its course...

Thimeo was 4 years old when I wanted him to be followed by a psychologist to compensate for the lack of a father and for me to confide in him. The first appointment with the psychologist took place on November 17, 2009.

For my part I didn't let go of Julio, I was angry and it was my right to want my son to have both surnames. He finally understood that I would leave him alone if he gave me that. So we met at the town hall on January 26, 2010 (I had made sure to make an appointment before noon so that he would be sober) in front of a public officer so that Thimeo could bear both our names...

A short time later I learned from Camilla that Julio had changed his address. He had been kicked out of the apartment because he drank a lot and had broken walls with his fists and his guitar... But Julio quickly fell back on his feet and he had found a new girlfriend, Arielle, on the Montparnasse side... I warned the bailiffs but again the doors remained closed. So still no recovery of alimony.

He still phoned from time to time to ask me about his son. He was about to leave for Iraq again and said he wanted to see Thimeo before he left but he never came. He also told me that he was going to pay the pension but I didn't see anything coming.

One day Julio finally stopped by the house. It was before a report in Afghanistan. He had come with a bottle of wine but he seemed fine and I decided I could leave him with his son for five minutes while I went downstairs to do the shopping. I thought Thimeo would be happy to spend a few minutes alone with his father... What a mistake! Just as I was about to pay, I got a call from Julio yelling at me to come home right away if I didn't want him to leave Thimeo alone in the apartment, that my son was a little jerk. I went back upstairs at top speed and when I got there I heard crying on the fire escape. It was Thimeo telling me that his daddy had kicked him out. I told him to stay there until I could get into the apartment and chase Julio out. Thimeo took a long time to console me, we had to go out for a walk and get some fresh air... When I came back, I realized that Julio must have drunk the bottle of wine in only five minutes.

Afterwards I became even more suspicious of Julio, with whom I never left Thimeo alone. And as he often didn't come when he was supposed to see his son, I finally decided not to warn Thimeo anymore to avoid the disappointment and the sadness that I read in his eyes at each withdrawal. For example, for his fifth birthday, on January 11th 2010, his father was supposed to come to celebrate his birthday at home, but he never came...

Our exchanges started to be done only by e-mail. I knew, still through Camilla, that it was not going well with Arielle, that he was regularly going crazy and that he had broken everything at her place too. She finally kicked him out of her house and Julio found a new girlfriend, Beatrice, with whom he moved in. It was a real headache because the procedures could never reach him, between his different addresses and the fact that he never took the mail.

Professionally, things were still working for me. In 2010, I made a documentary for Infrarouge and France2 with Jean-Michel Carré entitled "Sex, love and disability". I was very proud of it because I gave a voice to people who were never given one: disabled people who suffered from a lack of affection and love, and we revealed, thanks to the testimonies I had found, the existence of a profession that exists in some European countries, that of sexual assistant. Afterwards, I was entrusted with other subjects: I became a director for Endemol and the program "On a échangé nos mamans".

CHAPTER 7
WHEN THE GROUND COLLAPSES UNDER YOUR FEET

We had a well-established rhythm of life with my son, in spite of the legal worries that had made Julio change, in my eyes, from being a father to being a father. Camilla assured me that he had really loved me, that he had been faithful to me for some time, that he really wanted this child with me... but I remained in the incomprehension of such a behavior towards us and I was sad and pained for my son...

This relationship made me very unhappy. In fact, I remained single for most of Thimeo's childhood. And between work, which took up all my time, and my son, with whom I wanted to be on weekends, I had neither the time nor the desire to go out and meet someone.

My son, this little being full of promise, was growing day by day... Everything was new with him and he was making my life fulfilling... Alcohol at that time was very far from my thoughts and needs. I didn't lack anything: I had a beautiful son, I was working with celebrities, I had made a documentary and built my career without help from anyone. I was traveling a lot and I had a good salary at the end of the month.

In the summer of 2010, Julio wanted to introduce me to his girlfriend Beatrice to show me that he had found some stability with her. He wanted Thimeo to come spend a day or even a weekend at their house and to receive him at the same time as Melissa. He wanted to resume his role as a father a little. It was a jump that I didn't expect, but I was happy for Thimeo because I knew that he needed and wanted to see his father and his half-sister. As Beatrice seemed to me to be more settled and Julio a little more stable, I wanted to put aside my apprehensions so as not to deprive Thimeo of this reunion.

So I allowed him to go to his father and Beatrice's house, first for a few afternoons. Then, as my son seemed to be happy with these moments, I accepted that he could spend weekends there...

When I picked Thimeo up on Sunday night he was barely in the car and he immediately fell asleep, so I didn't know much about what they were doing. They were going to restaurants, having friends over in the evening... and Thimeo was playing with his sister, that's about all I knew. I only suspected that he stayed up late.

In January 2011, I learned from Camilla that Julio had gone for three weeks to a rest home at the very posh clinic of the Château de Garches... I was quite surprised, but I quickly knew that it was for alcohol withdrawal, which was a good thing. When he came back from the treatment, it seemed to have done him good, he seemed calmer and that reassured me.

From February, Thimeo started to go again to spend weekends at his father's, he even saw his grandfather Carlos with Beatrice and Melissa. But, nothing to do, I picked him up more and more tired and I didn't understand why.

The last time Thimeo went to Beatrice's house with his father and Melissa was the weekend of May 27-28, 2011. Afterwards, there was a catastrophe that I learned from Camilla: Julio had made his first suicide attempt, by hanging... They had just had a big fight and Beatrice had gone to the police station to file a report. She found him when she came back. He had relapsed and there was no question of leaving Thimeo with his father.

On Sunday, November 6, 2011, while Julio was away for a long time, Melissa called me and asked me to spend the day with us. I went to pick her up and we had lunch next to the Luxembourg garden, before going for a walk. When she heard that we had just adopted a cat, she wanted to come to the house to see it. When we got home, it was the end of the day. I let the kids play in Thimeo's room, and I started to prepare the meal.

The bedroom door was closed but I tiptoed over to see if everything was okay. I went back to my stoves until Melissa's grandmother rang to pick her up.

Thimeo and I sat down at the table and I asked him if he had a good day and what they had been playing in the room.

First he told me they had been playing spies... Then a few seconds later Thimeo cringed in his chair and told me, **"Mom, I lied to you;** we didn't play spies, Melissa asked me to lick her lisp." What a shock!!!

I didn't doubt his word for a moment, "lisp" was a word I had never uttered in my life. The ground slipped away from under my feet. Catastrophized, I told my parents and Camilla about it. I didn't sleep all night.

The next day I had to start a new job for a month, on which my intermittence depended, but I must say that my head was not in it. In the morning I phoned the shrink with whom we had an appointment the same evening. Thimeo told him everything and the shrink told me that he shouldn't see his half-sister anymore, that I should talk to the father as soon as possible.

So I gave Julio an appointment as soon as he came back from shooting, in a café next to Réservoir prod, at the Porte de Saint-Cloud, between noon and two. I said to him: "Listen, I have to talk about something very important. Something very serious has happened between Thimeo and Melissa...". But Julio was not in his right mind. He was speechless and didn't want to hear anything, he told me that he was going to talk to Michelle and Melissa about it and then he left.

Finally, the only feedback I got from him was that I was crazy. I, who was making sure that this story with Melissa was settled within the family, went to the police station in November 2011 to file a complaint against Julio for abandonment of the family, non-payment of alimony, and to ask that Thimeo not go to his father's house anymore... I turned to the justice system to protect Thimeo....

This resulted in a conviction against Julio on December 14, 2011 before the Criminal Court of Paris. Obviously, he did not receive the summons, the judgment that took place by default said this:

> "Whereas it appears from the elements of the file that the accused did not effectively discharge his obligations during the period referred to in the prevention, so that the family offence is established in all its elements... The court considers that there are grounds to declare him guilty of the facts of which he is accused and to pronounce a sentence of 6 months' imprisonment against him, taking into account his criminal record, his great casualness and the remarks made to the police showing a total lack of interest in his family obligations... "

> "On the public action declares Julio X guilty for the facts of family abandonment: non-payment of alimony for the facts committed from July 13, 2009 to April 9, 2010... Condemns Julio X to 6 months in prison."

And to pay damages to the civil party that I was. I only asked for the certificate of no appeal in 2012 because my goal was obviously not to have him go to jail. I just wanted Thimeo to not have to go to his father's house anymore, and to receive my alimony.

As I felt that my son was not doing well, I called a journalist friend who had worked on this kind of problem so that Thimeo could open up to someone he trusted and I could find out more. After speaking with Thimeo for a long time, this friend confirmed that my son was telling the truth. What he also told me was that this had been going on for a while, that if it hadn't been for that day with Thimeo and Melissa at home, it could have gone on for a long time... In fact, when Thimeo would go to his father's house for the night, his father would let the two children sleep in the same bed with a tablet. Melissa would force Thimeo to do all these things by telling him to shut up, threatening to make him sleep on the floor on the cold tile if he said anything.

This is proof that my son and I had a real trusting relationship for him to talk to me like that. He felt that it was not normal. Julio didn't care, he went back to Los Angeles to shoot, then to Syria with Beatrice.

On February 8, 2012 (Thimeo had turned seven a month earlier), the shrink told me that he was hesitant to report... I think he was afraid of the other family's reaction and we stopped seeing this practitioner who I didn't feel supported at all, and who wasn't helping my son.

On Thursday, March 8, we had our first appointment with a new psychologist specializing in EMDR[1], a method that I had been advised could apparently relieve trauma.

We went twice a week at first. I attended the sessions and I have to say that they were as hard on Thimeo as they were on me. I found out what my son had been through because the psychologist was reliving the scenes for him by mimicry.

------

1. Between hypnosis and cognitive behavioral therapy, EMDR is a psycho-neurobiological therapy based on sensory stimulation. Recommended by the World Health Organization, it helps patients to "put away" their traumatic memories in case of post-traumatic stress. This surprising technique has come to the aid of many survivors of the November 13, 2015 attacks.

She would use cars to represent Thimeo and his half-sister, and would bring in a police car to protect Thimeo... Once this was done, she would ask him to express his anger, he would start to cry, and then she would invite him to go into a rage, to break everything in the room, to throw cushions in all directions. Thimeo would come out of these sessions exhausted and so was I...

He understood that what had happened was serious. And I was discovering the scenes that he had lived.

As a result of all this, on Wednesday, March 14, 2012, as we were getting ready for dinner, I said to her:

- Thimeo, I know you're in pain, I know you're not well, but I've done everything I can, I've talked to your dad, who's talked to Michelle... We're seeing the shrink... But you see, nothing's happening... The only thing we can do now is go to the police.

He answered me right away:

- Mom, we're going to the police.

- OK. If it can relieve you, make you feel good, we go...

We left hand in hand to the police station of the 15th. It was not far from nine thirty when we arrived there, after walking twenty minutes in the night... To the policeman who came to ask us why we were there I answered: "I come with my son to file a complaint for incest." At these words we were immediately separated...

Thimeo's statement was shorter than mine. When he came to join me in the office where I was, he stood next to the policeman and looked at me and said, "Mom, now I know you are doing everything to protect me!!!". I will never forget that moment. *I still get teary telling that.*

The next day, Thursday morning, March 15, 2012, we had an appointment at the Brigade des mineurs, quai de Gesvres in Paris. Thimeo was very brave; there again we went hand in hand, plunging together into the unknown of the judicial administration. He was heard by the chief of the Brigade des mineurs, filmed... and his testimony left no doubt...

After a few days, Thimeo didn't want to go to school anymore, he was not doing well. I told him that everything was in the hands of the juvenile brigade, but I didn't know what to do. I didn't work anymore, I didn't speak with the father, the paternal grandparents were non-existent. I tried to call Colombia so that Julio's mother could talk to him, but nothing could be done, I was running into walls.

Moreover, I found myself in a total misunderstanding. Of the requested certificates, the one that was the most important for me was the one of Camilla, who claimed to be my best friend but who refused to give me one because "she didn't want to take sides for either one", between the father and myself, where it was only about Thimeo. I was deeply destabilized by her reaction because I continued to have her on the phone and to tell her everything. In fact, being Corsican herself, I think she didn't want any problems with Julio's family, and I know that she was always in contact with him.

CHAPTER 8
HOW ALCOHOL GOT INTO MY LIFE

In addition to all this, in April 2012, I learn, again from Camilla, that Julio made a second suicide attempt at Beatrice's house. She called the fire department and Carlos, the grandfather, asked for an involuntary admission to Henri-Hey Hospital and then to Sainte-Anne. I also discovered that Julio had been under the care of an alcohol specialist at Ste. Anne's for three years because he had been diagnosed with post-traumatic stress disorder (PTSD).

Of course I didn't talk to Thimeo about his father so as not to worry him... Time passed and my main job was to reassure him. I spent my days accompanying him to school, gathering the different procedures for non-payment of alimony, abandonment of family and collecting testimonies.

With this in mind, I contacted Arielle who, when I explained the situation to her, agreed to give me a statement. She told me that she had kicked Julio out of her house because he had broken everything. She was also in contact with Beatrice and she transferred me with her letter an e-mail of this one who told her to be beaten by Julio and to have suffered a lot too.

It was necessary for the procedure to collect all these testimonies but that was long and trying and was added to the appointments of Thimeo with the psychologist and mine, because I also needed it. I was also waiting for the phone call from the police station, the gendarmerie and the appointments with the lawyer.

But life went on as best it could, I went to pick up Thimeo from school, I helped him with his homework, I prepared the files... Then my evenings were spent putting away papers and making phone calls, searching on the internet... I, who was full of positive initiatives, a fighter on all fronts, discovered, painfully, what it was to wait for all this.

On Wednesday, May 23, 2012, I refiled a petition with the ALJ to protect Thimeo. The July 6, 2012 ruling said, *"It appears from the proceedings that Mr. Julio is currently being monitored for alcohol addiction and depression. He has in fact been hospitalized at the request of his father..."* Furthermore, following my complaint to the brigade of minors and according to the testimony of the psychologist who underlines that the clinical examination of Thimeo shows a great psychological suffering in connection with the sexual aggressions of which he reports to have been victim on behalf of his half-sister: *"It is necessary to contact that the situation is preoccupying and that Thimeo, seven years old, must meet his father in a secure environment."*

The judge also orders a psychological expertise of the parties, me, Thimeo and Julio. And reserves the father's right of accommodation.

This time was very difficult to deal with for another reason: I received quite explicit threats from Carlos and Michelle on my cell phone, which made my blood run cold. On the advice of my lawyer, I filed a complaint on July 14, 2012:

"I come before you today to report the following facts: in March 2012, I filed a complaint with the juvenile protection squad against Melissa, my son Thimeo's half-sister, for a suspected sexual assault she committed on my son.

The procedure is currently being processed by their services.

- I am coming to your services today at the request of my lawyer because I am being inundated with phone messages from the family of my son's half-sister, some of which are threatening to me."

"On 6/21/2012 at 5:17pm Ms. Michelle, Melissa's mother left me a message in which she threatened to come to my house and told me it was going to end very badly."

"On 13/07/2012 at 12:53 Carlos, Melissa and Thimeo's grandfather, upon learning of the complaint I filed against Melissa, told me that I was touching on something very, very sensitive and that in a Corsican family one does not file a complaint for this kind of thing...

"For my lawyer, these messages are messages of intimidation and she wants me to file a complaint for these facts.

(extract from the handbook)

Once that was gathered, I brought everything to the juvenile brigade and all I had to do was wait. Waiting for everyone to be heard and for the procedure to move forward, but it was no longer up to me. Waiting, always waiting. I couldn't cope anymore. Because in addition to taking care of Thimeo, of the appointments with the shrinks, I had to comply with the psychological expertise requested by the judge, which meant a lot of travel and availability.

So on July 19, 2012, to take our minds off things we went with Thimeo to New York for two weeks. We visited all the iconic places in the city. It was fantastic but he was still little, I hope he has some memories of it.

Then it was back to school in CE1 and the resumption of procedures and appointments...

The November 16, 2012 psychological expert report states: For Julio:

He says he didn't realize anything, that his daughter denies it... he talks about his follow-up for his alcohol withdrawal and says that he stopped taking any drug for 3/4 years. He mentions a suicide attempt and a compulsory placement in Sainte-Anne in 2012...

When the shrink hears Thimeo in the presence of his father:

Thimeo turns to his father and asks him if he still drinks.

"When you go on a trip, I was always afraid for you," Thimeo cries. "You never played with me..."

Finalizing their meeting Julio suggests that his son come back to Beatrice's house when Melissa is not there. "I'll tell Melissa not to come," but Thimeo replies, "I want Mom to be there."

The shrink notes that:

> "the conditions at the end of the exam where Julio becomes extremely sthenic with the expert constantly picking up on what he says and asking him to write down what he says in a very voluntary manner."

Mr. Psychological Profile:

> Mr. Julio is extremely defensive on examination and will sometimes become aggressive... Rigid and defensive posture which however covers a great psycho-logical fragility... Mr. Julio requires regular care to guarantee the psycho-affective supervision and the serene development of his son. Currently, Mr. Julio does not seek regular care and despite his hospitalizations, suicide attempts and known disorders, he does not see a psychiatrist and does not verbalize the recent events that focus as a father with his two children... so the simple reactivity of Mr. Julio in the presence of the expert is a sign of a worrying educational attitude...

About me:

> From his family relations, it emerges a lot of protection and complicity. Sometimes, the mother will take Thimeo to meet his father and take care of

the father's daughter. She is sorry to see the lack of relational interaction between them. She notices that her son Thimeo watches teenage movies at his father's house when her son is barely 5 years old... However, she adapts to the vagaries of the child's father's health so that Thimeo is not frustrated.

Psychological profile:

On examination, the woman is prolix, very present and even determined in her speech. She is clear in what she says and shows natural concern towards her son on the particular relationship with his father but also concerning the facts of sexual abuse and the ongoing complaint... Her concerns in terms of protection and education are supported by the description of Thimeo's malaise "lack of confidence, he didn't want to go to school anymore, tantrums..."

After investigation it seems imperative to separate Thimeo from his half-sister and to consider the maternal attitude as suitable.

Madam who always seemed to have a protective attitude towards her son...

About Thimeo:

Questioned alone and very calm, the child verbalizes very correctly for his age, showing a certain intellectual maturity.

Talking about his father, he said: "I'm always a little stressed when I go to see him. As soon as I see him, I'm less stressed and happy but it doesn't always end well.

One day he left me and called me names.

When I'm at Beatrice's, he doesn't take care of me, it's Beatrice or Melissa, otherwise nobody takes care of me.

He doesn't talk to me, I think he's a very unhealthy man. Melissa is used to it, I've never been used to it. I am afraid..."

Currently, "I feel better because I feel protected from Dad, Melissa, and all the people who hurt me by hurting my heart...Dad was either sleeping or drinking."

Asked about his activities with his father: "nothing".

Thimeo is a very mature little boy. Undeniably he showed signs of distress after the revelation before being able to verbalize properly and overcome the malaise in which he was.

Conclusion... Madam has asserted herself in a role of maternal protection and seems detached from the emotional imbroglio which bound her to the father of the child.

For the man it is necessary that he engages in a psychotherapeutic care in order to ask himself probably around the relations with his son the affective faults which constitute him beyond even a simple PDST (post-traumatic stress disorder). His disorders related to PTSD increase and testify to a probably old distress which should not influence the relationship with Thimeo....

Come 2013 and Thimeo is now eight years old.

The latest judgment of the JAF which is dated February 28, 2013 confirms that:

> *"Julio is not followed by any specialist in spite of his heavy past and a certain "psychological failure of the father"...*
>
> *In order for Thimeo to keep in touch with his father, this will be done through a mediated visit through an association."*

So I made an appointment with an association that was based on the other side of Paris so that Thimeo could see his father.

All this so that the first time he did not come and that the second time, while Julio had to be supervised by the staff of the association, he took advantage of a short absence of the staff to lift Thimeo's head and tell him to withdraw his complaint against his half-sister...

When I heard about this, I immediately contacted the association and suspended the visits for the sake of Thimeo. It was too much, I couldn't take it anymore, I started to lose my footing. And here is my downfall: no more papers to do, everything in the hands of the justice... I was tired, worn out and so full of sadness for my son...

So one evening while shopping before picking up Thimeo from school, without thinking, I bought a bottle of "buffalo grass", vodka. Unconsciously I knew that drinking would relieve me of the malaise I had been in for too long. Since

I never liked wine or beer, I turned to vodka, which is an odorless alcohol, and one glass of which would be enough to give me immediate relief. I guessed that it would take away the deep pain I felt for my son and myself for a few moments. I wanted to forget this whole period of sadness and suffering, or at least to lessen it.

When I got home I put the bottle in the freezer and went to pick up Thimeo from school.

We did his homework, he took his bath, and then I went to the kitchen. I poured myself a glass of alcohol at around 7:00 p.m... And then I immediately felt a huge relief. All the weight of what we were going through had disappeared and I found myself finally more serene, as if at peace. Alone in front of this trauma, which was also a little bit mine, I did not see the trap that was taking shape.

I started with a drink that made me feel like I was smiling and looking at life in a positive way with Thimeo, being a little more vibrant and happy, funny, leaving the problems behind.

I told myself that it was good for him to see me smile again, to be funny, to be present, not to have constantly this face catastrophized by all my concerns. I would put on the music, we would dance, but I was only hiding the misery and you can't fool a child. When you are sad, you are sad.

I didn't realize what I was doing, I was exhausted from all the years of fighting... I just wanted to lay down my arms, rest and then continue the battle. I had to find a way to relieve myself and I thought a little drink couldn't hurt... That was my biggest mistake.

CHAPTER 9
AN INTIMATE RELATIONSHIP WITH ALCOHOL

For a while I managed to maintain our rhythm of life: the outing to the square after school, the homework... We talked about his day, then to the bath! Then we would have dinner, read a story, and go to sleep with a kiss and an "I love you"...

It was once he was in bed that I took a second drink, just to breathe a little, like a breath at the end of the day. I would sit on the couch and feel calm... I could then tell myself that the hardest part was over, that I had to hold on for Thimeo but I felt really weak and down.

Then quickly, from one glass I went to two. Then to three while cooking... I was still able to keep up the illusion, except when I was on the phone and started talking about our long legal battle. Then I'd take another drink and get all worked up... I'd start to sink into the alcohol without anyone suspecting it, even for a moment. Not even me. It takes a long time to realize that you're an alcoholic... You can start drinking during the day, even when you're surrounded by your family, and no one would even suspect it.

In hindsight I understand why I chose vodka, which is a white spirit. It doesn't smell strong and in a glass, you can believe it's water. And then the relief effect is immediate. At the beginning, one glass was enough for me but I had to increase the doses quickly...

I thought I could hide my condition from my son by asking him to go to his room to watch cartoons or by going to the balcony to make a phone call so he wouldn't hear me. I continued to take him to the square but the vodka had replaced the water in the little bottle I took with me. I was trying to maintain a subtle balance between the apparent sobriety and the illusory well-being that alcohol gave me. I would watch Thimeo play, trying to stay sharp enough to make sure nothing happened to him. We would then go home and I would continue to take small sips of alcohol while helping him with his homework. Thiméo was doing well despite the absences that legal appointments imposed on him. I tried to maintain our rituals, baths, dinners, stories, but he was sleeping less well. He must have sensed that I was starting to be different and little by little, he found it harder and harder to wake up and started not wanting to go to school. In fact I think he knew very well what was going on because he had already experienced it with his father. I was just pushing him away from me.

But I didn't see him, I was submerged by my problems: the unpaid alimony, the psychological abuse of the father, the mourning of this relationship, the files to build, the photocopies, the calls to make, the steps to take, the changes of address of the father, the disaster of the incest, the sorrow of my son, the appointments with the shrinks, the associations... I really couldn't take it anymore...

On top of all that, I was suffering from not being able to do the job I had totally invested in. I was alone, I needed help, but I didn't want to accept my mother's help, who could see that things were not going well, but who still had no idea of the place that alcohol had taken in my life. Family is not always the best place to put words to these things.

However, I was not going to be able to pretend for much longer.

One Sunday, when the weather was nice and we were at my parents' house, I wanted to put up a bike rack I had bought to show my son that I was still there, enthusiastic and fit, but I knew I had had too much to drink. Once the equipment was almost in place, I ducked with my long hair and stood up too quickly: my eye hit the tip of the bike rack. I hurt myself badly and went to the hospital to make sure I hadn't damaged my cornea too badly... Obviously Thimeo was scared for me and I know that was one of the first obvious signs that I had fallen into alcohol and couldn't hide it anymore.

Maybe that's when I should have asked for help from my loved ones, that I should have consulted professionals, but I must admit that it didn't cross my mind... I didn't think it was going to escalate, I still told myself that it was just a bad patch, that I was stronger than the alcohol, that I would get back on track.

I was also less and less surrounded by friends, most of whom belonged to my professional network... On the phone they showed me compassion, but they could hear from my voice, from the way I spoke, that I was drinking. They didn't give me a second thought, but as time went on, the calls became fewer and fewer.

Chapter 9 An intimate relationship with alcohol

The vicious circle was well and truly in place. I needed to forget about it, so I drank every night... It was all too much for my shoulders and I was angry, very angry that I couldn't protect my son.

Perhaps this story of incest concerning Thimeo destroyed me even more because I knew what it was like to grow up without recognition of one's status as a victim... I saw myself as a little girl, sitting against the door of my room with a bottle of perfume in my hand to block my aggressor by throwing perfume in his eyes if he dared to enter my room: my maternal grandfather with whom I discovered pleasure in an unnatural way. I was eleven years old and it happened several times before I reacted. I told my parents about it and although they believed me, they didn't do anything for me at the time, especially since my grandfather had a stroke very soon after. So I built myself up by trying to "make it my case", but I didn't feel protected by my mother. It was a taboo thing at the time, just like today...

When I grew up, when I became a young woman with this in my head, I wished there was a court decision... Because it is not easy to build yourself with such a past...

If I always wanted to avoid the worst for my son, it was this one: to be sexually assaulted. I never thought that such a thing could happen to him one day... That's why I couldn't stand by and do nothing. I wanted him to be "recognized as a victim", that an investigation be made so that he could grow up serenely, build himself as a socially and romantically balanced teenager, that nobody could doubt his word... Especially since Julio's family now seemed threatening and dangerous, for my son and myself. It was necessary to go to the end and to hold in spite of everything...

I didn't know what kind of legal hell this would lead to, the consequences on my loss of control, my helplessness, my infinite sadness for Thimeo and for myself; all of this leading me directly to alcoholism... I didn't see that I was going to drown myself in glasses of alcohol to support all this and that I was going to lose my son. That my son was going to lose his mom...

I was already no longer a pillar to him. Some nights, Thimeo had to call his grandmother to pick him up from home and go to sleep at their house. This was very traumatic for him...

I would put on the television or tell him to go to his room, to leave me alone, but he could see that I was talking and crying on the phone, on the balcony... All the evening rituals were disrupted, I could no longer read him stories with the dynamic and passionate tone that I used to have. I always had a glass in my hand and the phone in the other, I was moving away little by little from the mother he knew, that's why he called more and more often his grandmother to ask her to come and get him.

I often ask myself these questions:

- Why did I start drinking when I had my son's full trust?

- If I hadn't done anything, would I still have been drinking?

- How would he have grown up? Would he have blamed me one day for "not doing anything"?

Wasn't the price too high? I think so... I don't know...

After several months, at the end of 2013, the juvenile brigade called me. It was the head of the investigation who told me that Melissa had admitted everything and that Thimeo was indeed a victim. That it had taken a long time because it had been complicated to get Michelle to come, as she did not want her daughter to be heard, and that the father did not come to the appointments…

As Thimeo was in his bath I asked him to call back in five minutes so that he could hear this from another voice than mine, it seemed important to me that Thimeo hear it from the head of the investigation. When he got the lady from the brigade on the phone, she told him everything: that he was a little victim and that he had nothing to blame, that his half-sister had admitted everything and that he had done the right thing by talking about it.

Thimeo hung up the phone and said, **"See, Mom, I'm glad you believed me, you did the right thing."**

There again my heart melted… But things were not settled because there was no court decision and I was already drowned in alcohol… The damage was done, and yet a judgment was still needed… I received a paper to go to court and file a civil suit for my son and myself but people around me advised me against it, they told me that I had to stop "stirring up shit". I knew that the procedure was still going to be long and for the moment I didn't have enough strength or courage for that… But it was coming.

The alcohol helped me to make this suffering bearable, it helped me to put my mind on "pause" for a few hours.

CHAPTER 10
FROM EVENING VODKA TO MORNING VODKA

Thimeo was in third grade, still at Saint Elizabeth. He was a very brave little boy, he made sure he stuck it out through all the storms we went through. I tried to take care of him as well as I could before the drinking, but I had gone from being a pillar to being an alcoholic mother. I drank every night, more and more... Almost a whole bottle... I even managed to bruise myself and cover it up with makeup.

But at least when I went to bed after drinking, I didn't think about our problems... I drank to fill myself with courage, and I didn't see the danger coming. No one saw it, or at least no one warned me: they didn't think I could be an alcoholic after all I had done, all I had been through. I was perceived as a strong and courageous person but it was the opposite, I was fragile and I drew a semblance of strength from alcohol. What an illusion! I let myself be carried away by this lie and I liked it.

As in this vicious circle I was not working, Thimeo was at school and normal people at work, I was bored and I spent the day wondering about the procedures that I found long and trying. Especially as I kept in mind that all my steps for the alimony remained silent: the CAF, the Treasury... nobody managed to touch Julio.

So I left my civil action for incest aside for a while. I didn't have the strength.

One morning, after having accompanied Thimeo to the school, I bought one or two flasks of vodka at a grocery store thinking to drink them in the evening but it was stronger than me: it was not midday that they were already finished...

From then on, drinking became my main occupation, along with the internet and TV. That's all I did all day until it was time to pick up Thimeo... On weekends, I tried to limit the amount of alcohol I drank so I could take my son to museums, the movies or Aquaboulevard... I tried to occupy the time in the best way, knowing that I was always thinking about the next drink I could have when I got home. Everything soon became an effort and I began to feel no pleasure outside of drinking. Drinking, however, made me feel like time was passing, I was constantly looking at papers but I was also tidying up, cooking, listening to music, dancing, taking my mind off things... The house was very tidy at that time! And of course, I bought vodka for the evening... Three flasks in the morning, three flasks in the evening.

Then I quickly switched to the big bottle in the morning, because it was cheaper and saved me a few trips to the grocery store. I always kept a flask to start the next day. No doubt about it: I had entered the infernal circle of alcohol... I spent my time on the phone and abandoned my son, I was much less attentive to him, less caring... Anyway, I was no longer caring for myself, how could I care for him?

I wanted to give Thimeo hope and make him understand that he had a family... So I started to organize, during this school year and with his agreement, his baptism.

This one took place on April 20, 2014, at the Saint-Lambert church in the 15th where I myself had been baptized. I made my brother the godfather of my son and Camilla his godmother and this, despite her past as Julio's mistress. She had witnessed my history with him and had become an important confidante for me. Even though she had not helped me when Thimeo was victimized, she had made me believe in a sincere friendship and she was kind to him.

I sent a simple email to Julio to let him know that he was welcome to attend the baptism of his son. He came and it was the one and only day in Thimeo's life where he was surrounded by all his family members. I'm not talking about Carlos who was not welcome or Melissa... For one day everyone put aside their resentments to be around him and celebrate him. To tell him that we loved him and to prove it by our presence. To show him that our love for him was the strongest.

I didn't drink too much to feel good that day. I did have a few flutes of champagne and some wine, but it wasn't 40% vodka!

Then my son understood before anyone else the reality of my condition and he asked his grandmother to pick him up at home one night, then two... This happened more and more often because I was no longer behaving normally. I didn't really walk straight anymore... When I went to pick him up from school I started false conversations and I didn't really listen to his answers... I tried to reassure him, but I wasn't convinced myself...

I see my mother again, sorry to discover me like this in front of the door and Thimeo who leaves without even saying goodbye to me, without looking at me... Apart from that I don't remember anything and yet this has happened many times...

Drinking every day had become a well-applied routine. I thought at the time that others didn't see anything, but I was wrong: in reality, people know and they keep quiet. I feel like I was left to sink into my own confusion. Only my mother tried to talk to me, but we were too close... It should have come from outside. I had a very paradoxical behavior, I was sending signals about my illness while not wanting to hear anything. I had to go to the end of my legal battle, to the end of myself...

Then I wanted to move, I couldn't stand life in Paris and its noise anymore. I needed some peace and quiet, to get away from the hustle and bustle that made my head spin.

I loved my apartment, but it held too many bad memories. What had happened with Melissa hit me every time I went into Thimeo's room. And since my parents needed money, selling the apartment seemed like the right thing to do. I can say now that it was in fact the worst decision I could have made: I destroyed my status and the Parisian life I had built up to enter a life of misery.

Chapter 11
From morning vodka
to the physical need for alcohol

I didn't feel able to do the job I used to do: I had so many problems myself that I couldn't interview people to listen and tell their stories. It became unthinkable to go on a shoot and leave my worries behind. I was tired all the time, worn out, and on alcohol...

Staying in Paris did not seem necessary anymore. The apartment I was living in was located at a crossroads and the noise was infernal. With the alcohol I had become more sensitive to noise and I could no longer stand this apartment where I had spent wonderful moments, in which I had put all my heart. My son's room was beautiful and made with love but it had become for me the room of the drama... and it was also in this apartment that everything had deteriorated: my addiction, my health...

My parents had taken a life annuity on their house in the Paris region because, although they had worked all their lives as shopkeepers, they had almost no pension and therefore no liquidity. Selling my apartment was thus a solution.

My life was changing and the infernal cycle of destruction continued. When I went out on the street, I had to walk along the walls because I was afraid of falling. I was losing my son's trust, I was leaving Paris... I was no longer the honorable person and caring mother that I had been.

So before the summer of 2014, I moved closer to my parents in the suburbs, in an apartment that had been difficult to find with a file like mine: without a contract of employment, intermittent of the spectacle, single mother, the father who never paid his alimony... I still ended up finding a furnished apartment without personality, in which I could not project us but which was five minutes from my parents' house. The school I had to put Thimeo in seemed cold... I think he was perfectly aware that a page was being turned... Nothing that I had built for us existed anymore. It could only get worse. Everything seemed gloomy, my status had changed. And all I could think about was alcohol.

In the morning I drank a little vodka, then I accompanied Thimeo to school, when he was with me because I was already taking care of him so badly that he often preferred to be with my parents. Then I would go and get alcohol for the day and evening. So I had it at home all the time and I drank all the time... I didn't feel like working anymore, I slept during the day and relied on my mother to pick up Thimeo most of the time.

It was obviously unbearable for Thimeo who had to learn to preserve himself from his mother and had to suffer a lot.

To keep him out of danger, I decided to move in with my parents. I was no longer able to be really present, to cook... I had no strength left for the two of us. I didn't have any strength for myself. No one was fooled: I got drunk from morning to night; my mother accompanied Thimeo, and I, as soon as I woke up, I drank. My rhythm had become this: beg, drink, smoke, sleep, beg, drink, smoke, sleep, beg....

I still remember the first time I had to beg my mother to buy me a bottle of vodka because I couldn't do anything without it... It was a morning when I woke up with sweaty hands, an indescribable headache and couldn't stand on my feet. I told my mother that you can fight a hangover with a glass of alcohol, even though I knew that the symptoms I was suffering from were more important than a simple hangover... She tried to reason with me but she could see that I was in so much pain that she couldn't help but accept what she didn't want to do: to go and get me a bottle of vodka in order to get rid of my pain.

It was always a long discussion to get her to go and get me some vodka but fortunately she went anyway. You can't understand the suffering of someone who can't drink any more when they are soaked in alcohol, but in those moments I couldn't even smoke a cigarette, all the sounds were multiplied by ten, my hands were shaking and my heart rate was high too, I couldn't stand up, I couldn't sleep, I couldn't stay awake... and in this state of withdrawal I still had to spend a lot of energy to get vodka!

Then my mother tried to hide the bottles to control my drinking... There is nothing more unbearable than being dependent like that, what's more from your mother, having to justify yourself when you can't say anything other than,

"GIVE, I NEED!" I know of course how much pain she must have been in when she gave in to me, but at that point nothing mattered more than finding a drink.

I was still aware of my drinking problem and that I had to do something about it... One of my first steps was to call Alcoholics Anonymous. This was not very successful as I was hung up on several times during the night when I was in distress and I was not rude... I didn't buy into the way they operated and felt no compassion. The people I ran into were preaching the good word but not hearing my pain. I know they helped a lot of people but for me it was a complete failure.

During the summer we went to the countryside in the Nièvre with my son and my parents, which did not change my habits: I continued to drink in secret. As there was always a bottle of my father's wine lying around in the kitchen, it made things much easier for me.

One day when we were arguing and I was pretty drunk, I wanted to take the car and leave with Thimeo. My parents had to hide him in the basement and they closed the gates of the house to prevent me from leaving with the car. I couldn't take my son but I drove through the fields. In the car I heard my phone ring, as it was a blocked number, I understood that they had called the police who were now trying to reach me. So I took some side roads, then stopped for a bit along the road to recover. I then drove on the highway to Paris with one eye closed because I was seeing double. I don't know how I didn't have an accident or cause one: I got home and fell asleep in bed.

Thankfully my parents had protected Thimeo, I had become a real danger to him. I could no longer ignore the fact that I had a real problem with alcohol. I was an alcoholic, that was a fact.

CHAPTER 12
THE ADDICTOLOGIST

Being aware of my problem with alcohol, I turned to an "alcohol doctor". The first one I went to see introduced himself as a former alcoholic. He was not judgmental, he put me at ease, telling me about himself, his separation... but I still had to tell my story again and I couldn't take it anymore...

I saw him once a week, but the only thing he did was tell me to stop drinking, for my own good, and prescribe me medication... I regret that I never met someone who would really talk about the problem of alcohol. I also regret, of course, that I didn't start treatment immediately, at the first sign... much sooner! While I had witnessed Thimeo's father's problems firsthand, I didn't see that I was replicating what my son had already experienced with him. All this while I was constantly trying to protect him from it!

It's a terrible thing to say, but when you're in alcohol, there's nothing else but that and the next time you can drink. Neither the doctors nor the hospital staff really understand how you feel... From a clinical point of view they know, but it is not enough and it is difficult to find a competent shrink. In reality, it is the life that we have that we must change. And forgive our wounds, learn to live with them. We are not told this enough.

And then this addictologist was down the street from my parents, on a street where there was a grocery store... I went alone to each consultation. During the five minutes it took me to get there, I would walk around thinking about my worries and that grocery store. I swore to myself that I would not stop there on the way back, I wanted to get better, to say no to alcohol! I wanted to get out of it! And then I told my life story once again and my addictologist told me that I had to stop drinking to find a life with my son, that at the moment I was not taking care of him and that he was giving me the cold shoulder... I cried for thirty minutes in his office, I confided in him with all the tears of my body, I told him about all the miseries we had gone through, my son and me...

He would prescribe me medication, but when I left his house, my feelings, pains and sorrows were so great that it never failed: I would go to the grocery store and pick up at least three or four flasks, one of which I would drink immediately.

I couldn't help it: even if my heart and my head said no, my body needed it. My head and my heart were not deciding anymore. My brain was disconnected and all I could think about was alcohol, drinking to forget all this suffering once again.

Where is the *trigger*? This famous *click* that I had heard about in shows about alcoholics, and that the doctor told me about. What does it look like? How does it happen?

I was finding ways to bring alcohol home, I hid the flasks in my pants or I stuck them in my boots... I did this for a while to avoid my mother to go and get some for me. After a while, seeing that it didn't get any better, my mother started to accompany me to the addict's. I had to convince her that she could not go to the addict's. I had to convince her that I had to stop and buy some vodka, I succeeded because she could see that physically it was the only thing that made me feel better.

I had read that you can die if you are in withdrawal from alcohol. Professionals contradict each other on this subject but what is certain is that the state of withdrawal is unbearable and very real... Abnormal palpitations, cold sweats, trembling, crying, your whole body shakes from the inside, the noises are all too loud, you can't talk anymore, you can't even watch TV, you can't follow. You really feel like death is imminent. Then at the first drink - a good one, not a ridiculous drop - well then everything gets better... All the symptoms disappear.

One day the addictologist explained to my mother that until I was ready to stop, I would always find a way to get alcohol but that it could be dangerous with medication. He preferred that I drink until I was willing to go into treatment for withdrawal. So we talked about what alcoholism was. He explained that it could only come from me, that the physical withdrawal was real, and that even medication was no match for the alcohol. My mother tried to understand. He then recommended a clinic with a specialized addiction floor. While waiting to get in, I was allowed to continue drinking. He said to my mother, "Keep buying alcohol for your daughter until she is taken care of... It's better to do that than to mix it with drugs and alcohol..." Poor mom, I put her through a lot too! You destroy yourself and your family...

Of course, one does not enter these centers immediately. We know that you can die from alcohol just by falling, but the wait is three weeks for a simple pre-registration appointment to see if you are fit to enter the service. That's too long... The worst disasters can happen while waiting.

We finally received a phone call for an appointment at the Saint-Cloud clinic at the Four Towns Hospital with the person in charge of admissions...

My God, how creepy it was! On the first floor there was a poor tree all alone, a small coffee stand with a not very friendly lady... It looked like a hospital about to close... And we didn't understand anything the gentleman in charge of the entrances was saying... I nevertheless told him about the critical situation in which I was and my motivation to enter care. He told me that since there were only twenty beds, it would take two to three weeks before a place became available.

We came out of the office and the walls were gray, disgusting, it was really sad to death... So much so that my mom and I had a nervous laugh! But it was important to keep things in perspective: if coming here could get me off the booze, then I was going to get on that train on my way to recovery!

When I got out of there, I bought a bottle of vodka with my mom next to me... It was supposed to be one of the last. I drank it glued to the car seat because I was so craving it.

Afterwards, with the withdrawal, my body would no longer be in physical need of alcohol... A deliverance was coming.

In the meantime, we went to see the family doctor one morning. I insisted on getting out of the car and going into the waiting room while my mother parked. I actually knew there was a supermarket where I could buy alcohol. I took a big bottle of vodka and poured it into a bottle of water in the middle of the street. When I arrived in front of the doctor's office, I drank the 75 cl in two minutes. Then I went in the waiting room where my mother joined me, and while we waited for our turn I felt that it started to rise...

The doctor received us... and I went into an alcoholic coma. I passed out in his office and I woke up in the Antoine-Béclère hospital, in Clamart... My mother, with tears in her eyes, holding my hands... I wanted to go out, but we had to wait a long time for the doctor... On the way back, I begged my mother to stop and buy a bottle of wine, which she firmly refused at first. I took three pills, but in my head I wanted alcohol and nothing else, I hated it at that moment.

Then I started to walk the dog in the street and of course I took the opportunity to go to the grocery store, I hid the bottles everywhere again, in my pants, in my boots... I never stopped drinking.

Chapter 13
First time in an addiction center

And then the big day arrives, in November 2014.

The day I went to the hospital for what was to be my one and only withdrawal. I was going in the same way one goes into a hospital to have a tumor removed and come out completely cured. I didn't see Thimeo, who was staying with my brother, before I left. He was avoiding me anyway...

We arrived at the hospital of the 4 cities in Saint-Cloud. I had drunk a flask of vodka before going there, with the agreement of my parents. It is indeed common to drink before entering this kind of place.

The withdrawal is to last two weeks and I take it very seriously, I know that this is an opportunity that I must not let pass.

My parents accompany me to my room and say goodbye. We are all very moved, aware of what is at stake.

I have a single room, reduced to the bare minimum: a bed, a rolling table for trays, a desk and a chair, a bathroom with a toilet. The nurses inspect my things: blood test, blood pressure test, an infusion for two days and then they give me Valium. I was already feeling better.

Here everyone knows each other and no one judges anyone... We've all been through critical situations, no matter what the product. Alcohol is the big winner, it has affected everyone. I quickly know that so-and-so is on his fifth withdrawal, that another has done eight and three six-month cures...

We are three young women among a majority of men, from 25 to 55 years old on average. The young women are quite withdrawn. One was a victim of incest and started drinking and smoking cannabis. The other, of Congolese origin, drank mainly rum. She often changes her mood, confronts boys to assert herself and taxes a lot of cigarettes. People avoid her because they suspect her of stealing food from the rooms. Among the men, the younger ones are there because they drink liters of 8.6 in addition to smoking cannabis. Some of them have integrated the withdrawal by decision of the judge. For the older ones it is mostly people who have to stop drinking because of health problems due to alcohol, mainly cirrhosis to various degrees...

What is destabilizing is that out of the twenty or so of us, most of them are not in withdrawal for the first time... In addition to being discouraging, seeing all these lives destroyed by alcohol scares me. It's like this famous *click*... Where is it for these people who laugh at being in withdrawal? I don't detect deep inside them a real desire to get out of it, because the environment they live in... because they went too far... because they like it, the alcohol, the dope... They know that once they're out of there, they'll go back to their routine and their addictions...

And then we take care of them here and it's true that in this micro-society they feel they exist a little more, they feel considered, which is not the case outside. Some of them spent so much money on alcohol that they could not afford to eat properly. So coming to withdrawal means being taken care of from a medical point of view and getting back to a rhythm of eating. It's a semblance of life in this medical environment.

If we don't drink anymore in these centers, we smoke a lot more. It must be said that there is nothing else to do. Some even smoke joints, others exchange drugs and smoke them.

For my part, I tried to keep a little distance by concentrating on myself and by resting as much as possible... But very quickly, alone in your room, you get bored. It's okay for the first few days, when you arrive and you can barely stand up, but after five days you're running around in circles. The day is punctuated by the distribution of medication and meals as well as cigarette breaks. We have almost daily appointments with the doctor who comes to each room in the morning. We talk with him for ten minutes about the analyses, the lack, what we feel, the treatment and the effects of the medication, then he adjusts the treatment according to what we tell him, our mood. It's the one appointment of the day that you don't want to miss.

During this first withdrawal I found the nurses calm and welcoming, I was surprised to see the patients laughing and that everyone was on first-name terms... There are bursts of laughter during the day and confidences in the evening when we hear people lamenting their fate. We share things about our lives and the consequences that alcohol has had on us, what made us fall, what we were taking, at what rate... We tell what we want. Anyway there is no shame in it, we are all here for the same reasons or almost: the excess of alcohol and other substances for some.

Chapter 13 First time in an addiction center

However, we all come from different backgrounds: I, after having tried to be a good mother, to protect my child, to have worked a lot and to have earned my living, I found myself with 100% care and on the RSA, with my son whose parents, wanting to preserve him as much as possible from my illness, gave me very little news...

Knowing all this, I didn't want to tell my story again... The main thing in these meetings is not to reveal too much, and to say as little as possible... If you stay a little on the sidelines, people don't come and bother you too much. Some people respect the distances or the desired moments of solitude, and when this is not the case, you have to reframe immediately.

I understood later on that therapy is mostly done between patients, that you have to know how to listen because we have all arrived at the same place and that for some it is neither the first nor the last time. Therapy is done as a preparation for the next relapse. As if it was a bit in the order of things. It must be said that the product that makes us sick is accessible everywhere, that it is almost impossible to resist it and thus to get out of it...

One day an older lady came in, she was on her sixth withdrawal here. She was ashamed and didn't know how she was going to get through it. She knew all the staff and how the facility worked. She smoked very little but would go out into the stairwell anyway to get some fresh air. She knew her journey was endless and cried constantly. As soon as she returned home, she would relapse, until she no longer went out and had her alcohol delivered to her home.

She was a very nice lady, quite fine and elegant, who lived in Versailles. Miraculously, she did not have the head of an alcoholic, but she lived alone, her children did not want to see her anymore. It was only thanks to her neighbor, who had called the fire department several times, that she was still in this world. This woman did not want to go to treatment because she did not want to be away from home for too long. For her, withdrawal was the only thing that mattered. I was one of the only people she would talk to because I was gentle, calm, and a little bit distant and she felt she could confide in me. I think it did her good to confide in me about her confusion. On the other hand, I thought that if a woman with her experience and education could not manage to get out of it, it would be very difficult for me...

There are also activities that you can take part in once a week: theater, drawing, discussion groups... The problem is that alcohol attacks the neurons so much that the joints, the muscles, the brain can no longer function normally... And let's face it, for the majority of patients, learning how to make bookmarks or mandalas is not going to get them out of alcoholism... One day I felt like I was in kindergarten: we had two booklets with food groups and little stickers that had to be placed on them... And the lessons on nutrition are very good but once is enough. Before and after each activity it's the cigarette break, then we breathe something else than the hospital smells, paradoxically it's there that "we take the air"!

All these moments are very important but I think we all know that it is only an "aside" in our lives... A time of rest for the body and for the soul, surrounded by benevolent nurses...

We know that this does not heal the evil that we carry within us and that will always be there when we leave the center.

I believe that it is the psychiatric follow-up that is missing in these withdrawals. It's absurd that this part is neglected, as if society wants us to relapse... And when you see the price of rooms for a night in some establishments, you have to admit that it's a real business. Especially since these places do not empty since relapses are an integral part of the alcoholic disease, as the doctors themselves say. For some, it takes longer than for others, but for all, the circle is infernal to get out of it. Some people spend their time going through withdrawals and relapses, it becomes an assumed way of life... People eat better than at home, they are surrounded, there is medication and they are completely taken care of: this rhythm of life can suit them perfectly... and all this at the expense of the social security! The system is flawless: you drink, you pay taxes on alcohol, you go for a withdrawal or a cure at the expense of the health care system, you drink again, you pay taxes, you die, and no more pension to pay!

All strata of society are there: from the richest to the poorest. There was a former company director who had lost everything and had started drinking. He came to rehab for his wife who was still at his side. Another had fallen into alcohol little by little by drinking on the job. He spent his time drawing and was very talented but didn't mix too much with others.

The young people were mainly unemployed and spent their time drinking in poor neighborhoods with friends without thinking about the consequences for their future... Anyway, most of them could not really project themselves in a nice future, with already records for drug use or possession, and sometimes a stint or two in prison... So yes, what future for them? They preferred to laugh about it and accept their destiny, already written according to them.

Fifteen days like that, listening to each other's drinking stories... We create brief affinities that don't often last, the desire to forget this bad moment being the strongest.

I didn't want Thimeo to come and see me because these places are forbidden to minors. I didn't have him on the phone either because my parents wanted to protect him. I don't know what they told him about me... The truth is, I think I was taking care of myself...

After weaning two choices exist:

- A cure of one to six months in places that we have heard about during our cigarette breaks and that have a bad reputation, that are too far away and for a treatment that lasts too long...

- Going back home, which is dangerous because the drinking reflex can return very quickly. Very, very quickly.

For me, rehab still meant being removed from society, from real life, from my family... And if after two weeks, my body was no longer addicted to alcohol, the problems that caused me to drink were still there... It seemed to me that removing myself from society for one or six months would not change anything. I was tired of it. I believed in myself.

During these two weeks, an association of former alcoholics came to speak to us late one evening. They hardly mentioned the alcoholic nightmare but rather insisted on: "How good it is to live without alcohol!" They say "that they have no problem to see the others drinking", "that one day they had the famous *click*"... and when we try to know what this *click* is, they speak to us about the association, that it is necessary to come... In short. This gives the strange impression that they are just happy to come and talk about themselves, that they are not doing it for the others... These meetings are depressing for those who attend: there is nobody there, the few people who are present drink their tea without showing any real interest... And the speech of these volunteers is no longer adapted to the population of the centers which has evolved. The problems, the way of consuming alcohol is not the same anymore...

In any case, I didn't get the *trigger from* their contact and I didn't find it during withdrawal!

When the withdrawal is over, we say goodbye to everyone, we all know each other, we exchange a few phone numbers (which we should not do). We wish each other courage. The luggage is ready from the day before, it is necessary to make the papers, we wake up at seven o'clock but we cannot leave before ten or eleven o'clock... We hope never to return and the nurses tell you:

- I hope this is the last time we see you!

- Yes, so am I!

Chapter 14
Back Home

Upon returning home in early December 2014, my relapse was both easy and unexpected.

By chance, I found a full bottle in my bedroom closet... My mother had cleaned up, searched so that this wouldn't happen.

I had found Thimeo again, but you can't erase months, years of drinking in two weeks... He was angry with me and I understood that, so I tried to leave him alone instead of going to him. I knew I had to let him come back to me, that he needed time and proof, but just seeing him run away from me made me feel discouraged and the sadness never left me. The alcohol was the strongest. At the sight of the bottle I couldn't resist... The reason, the love of your loved ones, their disappointment if you start drinking again... All that disappears, you don't even think about it for a moment when the alcohol box in your brain opens again. It's inexplicable given the stakes. There is also the notion of the forbidden that is exciting to cross. I learned later that specialists advise against "tracking" an alcoholic, yet at that time, the slightest of my actions was observed with a magnifying glass... And it's true that succeeding in deceiving one's world, one's closest family who is watching you, and obtaining alcohol, drinking it, hiding it, saving it for later... It gives one great satisfaction! I used to wait for my parents to go to the garden or to do the shopping and I would quickly go to my room to drink from a bottle that I had carefully hidden in unlikely places like behind photo frames or in the hoods of my coats...

After those two weeks of withdrawal, I was feeling better so my parents let me go to the addictologist alone, but I went back to the grocery store.

It soon became apparent that I was drinking again, and there it was again: in agreement with the addictologist we made a new request for withdrawal. This was followed by three weeks of waiting and alcoholism, nightmares for my parents, and for my son who continued to avoid me by going to his uncle's house often. I also avoided him because the physical withdrawal symptoms soon returned. I didn't want him to see me, unable to take a cup of coffee without shaking if I didn't have my vodka fix. My mother rationed but it was hell... I had to justify a need, vital at the time, and endure guilt-inducing phrases such as: "it's up to you"... Ah, if only it were so simple!

There was my son, his failing father, Camilla whom I avoided calling because I didn't want her to tell Julio about my life... It was a vacuum around me, except for the alcohol that was always there, the alcohol that I could always count on.

I also realized that it was harmful to stay in contact with people in withdrawal or rehab. At the beginning it can be good, but very quickly you get calls from drunk people.

For example, some time after I left, while I was falling off the wagon, a man from the withdrawal called me and told me that he was doing great, that he was in the forest walking his dog, that he had gone back to his parents' house in the country and that no, he had not relapsed, that he only allowed himself a beer every now and then.... And then follows a phone call at 11pm, completely drunk and sad. I said to him: "Listen, it hurts me to hear you like this, but I can't do anything for you, I'm not a psychologist..." This produces a very painful mirror effect. In addition, we lie about our condition, we hide our relapse... How can we do something for the other person when we are unable to do it for ourselves?

"I treat myself, I relapse, I treat myself, I relapse..." The course was well underway and I didn't know how to get out of it with this alcohol available everywhere, like a miracle cure to forget one's problems.

I was going to my appointments with the addictologist and psychologist twice a week before the second withdrawal that was to begin on February 12, 2015 at the same location in St. Cloud. I was obviously still drinking and my mother was the only one who put up with my problem, tried to understand it and show compassion for me. I didn't take the medication because I knew that the mixture was dangerous. With the alcohol it seemed like I was in control and the effect was really immediate. That was what I needed.

Three weeks later, I returned to the Four Towns Hospital. Some people had left, others had already returned, but the problems were always the same: company managers, alcoholics who had to stop drinking for their liver. And lost young people, rather proud of their excesses whereas at their age I remember that I wanted to bite life to the full.

I put my head down, ashamed to be in this state again and to have relapsed as I had almost been predicted. The difference was that I was on the other side of the fence, and when asked "Is this your first time here?" I had to answer that it was my second time and that didn't surprise anyone...

A feeling of despair floats in the air at this answer among the smokers... We no longer stand out in the system, our number adds up, we are part of the old.

During withdrawal, you ask yourself a lot of questions and you know the answers. In my case, I knew that if what happened to Thimeo had not happened and all that followed, I would not have started drinking and I would have continued to work at my job while taking care of my beloved son. I was also aware that while this new withdrawal would allow my body to rest from alcohol and fill the void in a medical setting, it would not be the answer to my personal problems...

They are so important, I am so deep in the abyss that I hardly want to open my eyes... or at least to think about it, to talk about it... I observe, I take my pills, I sleep and I smoke. Enough of other people's problems, I have to think about myself, to rest as much as possible.

So when I was offered a treatment in Royan, I filled out the application form to get in quickly in order to avoid any relapse and try to really get out of it. I was weaned, so I didn't have any physical withdrawal from alcohol, but I was under the effect of powerful drugs to keep me going.

CHAPTER 15
ONE MONTH TO REBUILD? REALLY?

This is my first treatment. It is March 2015, in a pretty bourgeois house, in Royan, fifteen minutes from the coast. We breathe the good air of the sea, of the Atlantic.

Welcomed by the director of the establishment, you have to sign a kind of moral contract by which you certify that you are weaned. This was my case: I was only on medication and I respected the treatment.

The gates remain open but there is no question of playing the fool: you can only go out, accompanied by elders, during the second week, and then on your own during the third and fourth weeks... If you are caught drunk, and the analyses confirm it, you are excluded and you have to leave by the first train. It happened to one of us who went out the day he arrived and came back drunk. Some of the older staff saw him on the terrace and reported him... He left the same evening.

It was a beautiful day in March and there were many people smoking in the garden in front of the pavilion when I arrived. Everyone was looking at me, I was the newcomer, it was quite strange. On my side I saw only lost souls, aged and damaged by alcohol or other. However, in reality it was the new ones who were sad and depressed, the old ones seemed to be in good shape and looked happy to be there. But again, it is a cure, it is not "real life". We are separated from the rest of the world, protected from ourselves and our alcoholic impulses.

You always find the same profiles in this kind of establishment, whether it's for withdrawal or for treatment, even if each story is different. The people who were in Royan came from all over the world, from Lille, Paris, Brittany... As in the case of withdrawal, there were more men, young or old, than women... And the latter were older. Their alcoholism had been going on for years and now their family circle was pushing them to treat themselves. For some, their health required a total and definitive stop of alcohol.

So I was going to have to spend a month there, just with two hours of phone a day and no TV, only a library. For rest, it's not bad, but for healing, is it really the solution? But I was motivated and I was looking forward to see what was going to be offered to me... It was an introspective cure, so I was eager to know more and to start the process.

There were two of us per room and we were color coded according to our arrival date. For the meals, the tables were composed of two old people approaching the exit, two people who arrived three weeks ago, two people who arrived two weeks ago and two new arrivals. This makes it possible to be quickly integrated and made aware of the functioning of the center. Once again, we know everything about everyone right away: "He's here for alcohol, he's here for drugs". But the majority of the opinions were rather positive about the establishment and I was happy to have chosen this cure.

The staff is relatively limited, it is the "curists" who set the table, prepare the dining room, clean up, sweep the room... We are not allowed to use the cell phone during the day, but only two hours after dinner and before bedtime... It is up to us to go and get the pills and I will soon discover that we have to be the first to get them, otherwise we have to stand in line and that's long. In the evening, as we didn't have a TV, we read or smoked our cigarettes accompanied by an herbal tea until it was time to go to bed.

Most of them had already been here and had planned it, they had two phones, one they gave and one they kept. Here again I had the impression of a real industry, because, I repeat, the people are taken care of by the health insurance, by the mutual insurance company, and they meet in cure between buddies, they are made to eat, they are given medicines, some cheat with hash and alcohol (the controls do not take place every day and when one makes the turn of the garden, one discovers corpses of bottles...)

The treatment did have a purpose, however, and we had classes in NLP (Neuro Linguistic Programming). NLP is a set of communication and self-transformation techniques that focus on our reactions rather than the origins of our behaviors. It focuses on the how rather than the why, and proposes an observation grid to improve our perception of ourselves and others. It also allows us to set goals and achieve them. It is a toolbox, the key to which lies in the language and the use that each of us makes of our five senses and our body.

Its purpose is to allow you to program and reproduce your own models of success. It is very interesting because it is an introspective work. We know why we are here: to reflect and question ourselves, to understand why we started drinking. To find and have this famous *click*.

With each class, we found ourselves smarter and more educated for having been able to learn about the workings of our brains and understand reflexes with alcohol that we didn't know we had.

One of the first classes brought together all the newcomers: twelve who had arrived that week, including me. We had been assigned the color yellow.

We were put in a room where one by one we had to tell our story in front of everyone so that we could get to know each other better, why we were here, and what level our alcoholism was at. This was supposed to be private to the group, supposedly. Let's move on.

It was sad and pathetic, all these sufferings and problems related to alcohol in one room, all these people so different who had in common only the comfort they found in alcohol. One would pass them on the street, one would not imagine...

We also had classes on alcohol, on the diseases that are related to it. We also looked at our alcoholic genealogy to study the different habits of the people in our family and to see to what degree they drank alcohol... We used graphs to see the distribution of people who drink around us and in what way in order to identify how much alcohol surrounds us. This allows us to avoid pitfalls later on by better analyzing risky situations. In this respect, this treatment was really beneficial to me because I understood a lot about my family.

I was not aware that my family was so connected to alcohol: my grandfather was a great drinker, my father drinks every day, at noon and in the evening... My parents' friends too... All my former entourage...

We know that it is not good to drink, but once you are in it, it is the only thing that makes you feel good... We know that we can die from it, but as long as we don't have this famous *trigger*, alcohol is the best solution... We already know that alcohol is bad, that it destroys families, and I was very well placed to know how much since I no longer had a link with my son, whom my parents protected from me.

For the last week at the spa, four of us wanted to have lunch outside. This lunch was a real test, we had been told so much about alcohol that we were afraid of cracking!

It was very strange, after the confinement, to be left alone, even accompanied, when you felt so protected in the center. I can't even imagine what it must be like after a treatment of several months... I believe that one should not remain too long isolated from the world that continues to turn.

By a beautiful sunny day, we found a good restaurant, facing the sea... A beautiful white room, pure and stylish with a beautiful glass roof... We all ordered a dish, and for the drinks it was variable, fruit juice or "a syrup with water, please"... We were proud of us, of these four weeks spent

Two young couples arrive and talk with the waiter. A few moments later, the waiter comes back with a bottle of water... What a joy to see that we could go to the restaurant and order water as other young people did. But a few moments later, it is cocktails for the girls and whisky for the boys that the waiter brought... We had a strange feeling: these good moments were thus prohibited to us?! For ever? The prospect alone was unsettling. We had to be different for life from the others who could drink alcohol? It was a difficult realization.

The *click* was still far away... I had a feeling of despair even if the bet on our side was successful.

At the end of the cure I found my parents who had come to get me with Thimeo. He saw me in good shape, but he was a little distant, distrustful, he did not understand why his mother was sick.

I had no choice but to introduce him to two ladies who were nice but who, even sober, carried their years of alcoholism with them. I think Thimeo realized that. He didn't understand why I was with people like that and yet... That was my place at the time.

I would have had to find him outside the center. Maybe our reunion would have gone better... Thimeo didn't understand the disease, he experienced alcohol as an abandonment on my part and he was right, because between the periods when I was at home on alcohol and we avoided each other, and my passages in withdrawal and in rehab, his mother was always absent... He had only a shadow of a mother immersed in the hell of alcohol. Thimeo couldn't understand. Or nobody really explained it to him.

I hoped that our relationship would improve after this treatment, since I was fit and back to my old self... But the turmoil of the past does not fade so easily in the head of a child who was traumatized and almost abandoned by the alcoholism of his mother, who had been so loved until then.

Chapter 16
The Corsican expulsion

So I went out in April 2015 and, taking advantage of the vacations, my mother had booked for the four of us - me, my parents and Thimeo - a week at a club not too far from Royan.

It was supposed to allow us to turn the page, but it didn't work with my son anymore... He was sulking, didn't want to go out and refused to go with the other children... And then there was this double authority in which he certainly had a hard time finding his place, between a mother who had just come out of rehab and a grandmother who had been taking everything in stride for many months... I was ashamed and I was on medication, I didn't dare or know how to take back my place as a mother.

On the other hand, it's hard to see others drinking in front of you at first and my father would open a bottle at every meal... The pain it caused me told me that it hadn't gone away. I wasn't cured and my son must have felt that I hadn't gotten the *hang of it,* even though I hadn't been drinking during that rehab, nor during that dreary, rainy week that didn't bring us together or make us forget our problems.

When we returned to Paris - *weaned, curated* - despite the tensions I put on a brave face while still being sad in my heart. I knew and measured the harm I had done to Thimeo, to my parents and the time lost.

I couldn't see myself living in that new apartment and I knew that Thimeo didn't want to be there alone with me... The alcohol clouded my mind so much that I can't remember whether or not we tried to move back in. What is certain is that we quickly went back to my parents and I to the addictologist... and in the process to the grocer...

In the early summer of 2015, even though I was still drinking I was still feeling the benefits of the cure: I was drinking all day but less and I was holding my liquor again.

With the summer vacations coming up, Camilla invited us to spend two weeks in Corsica at her family home.

We took the plane together and when we arrived there we went shopping at the supermarket. Camilla with Thimeo, and me on my side. I bought two three things necessary for the meals and I obviously jumped on the opportunity to buy two bottles of vodka.

I knew that Thimeo's godmother was rough, that we were under her authority from Corsica and that I would not have my place as a mother here either. It made me uncomfortable, especially since when Thimeo was a victim of incest, Camilla was the only one who didn't give me a statement because she didn't want to "take sides"... She hadn't taken any interest in me when I went for treatment either. She had disappeared from the screens of my phone only to reappear for Thimeo... I felt that I didn't really matter to her anymore. For ten years she had taken the place of a trusted confidante, but what were her interests? I had never asked myself the right questions until then...

In Corsica, I didn't feel comfortable with her, and we were going to the house of her parents who had just passed away a few months before... It wasn't very cheerful... Once again, alcohol seemed to be the solution, it was there to give me the courage to stay and to try to be accepted in "her community"... to which she didn't hesitate to talk about my alcoholism. How could I feel comfortable and accepted?

It was a small village perched on the side of a mountain, where everyone knew each other. The house was immediately invaded by people from her family who had cleaned for her. She showed me my room, which was her parents' room... As soon as I was alone in there, I opened my first bottle to "breathe". I drank like that for two days, taking small sips as soon as I could, to support this stay.

One day we went to the beach, and Camilla put Thimeo in the front seat, while I was in the back seat of this little car, encumbered with a huge buoy. My place should have been next to her, of course. But, she who never wanted to be a mother, I felt that she was taking advantage of the situation and that Thimeo was playing her game. She was so proud to be the godmother of Julio's son that she usurped my place as mother by giving her permissions that should have come from me.

She kept talking to Thimeo, I tried to take part in their conversations, to impose myself but it was not easy. She never left me alone with my son, we couldn't spend a minute together. She would walk me around...

Then there was a market in the village, I had a couple of glasses of wine, and bought a local liquor which I started to drink too. Thimeo had made some friends and was playing with them, so I went home to bed, which must have tipped Camilla off. The next day she waited for me to go to my room to drink and then caught me in the act. She then went through my things, found the bottles and made a monumental scandal... Within seconds the whole village knew about it. Her demonstration was not intended to spare Thimeo, whom she hastened to take away from me by taking him to a nearby house. I did not see him again until I left, I could not even say a word to him, to apologize... However I was only pain and suffering. I didn't understand the reaction of this woman who had called herself my "friend". She didn't mince her words, it seemed like this was what she was waiting for and that I had pleased her.

As mistress of the house, she chased me out of her house, without trying to understand, without talking to me, without any compassion, and without offering me a second chance. She asked me to take my things and sent me back by the first plane, forbidding me to take my son with me, under the pretext that he would be much better off on vacation with her than with me.

And me, her friend in all this, understanding, empathy, forgiveness? And that, of course not, that doesn't serve as a *trigger* either.

It was a split; this woman who played a double role, sleeping with Thimeo's father for years, who pretended to be my friend, who witnessed all my disillusionments, my confidante... I was just waiting for some warmth and understanding, but she never helped me. I haven't heard from her since that summer when she kept Thimeo for three weeks. She refuses to talk to me, never gives me any news about my son when he is with her and does nothing to bring the family together and unite around Thimeo for his sake.

I made this woman the godmother of my son but the only thing she was interested in was to have an impact on me to be close to the Corsican family on my father's side. A few years later, in December 2018, I phoned the priest of St. Lambert Church, where Thimeo was baptized... I explained the situation to him, which he understood very well, and he removed Camilla's name from Thimeo's baptismal certificate...

Normally, in the eyes of the law, the godmother has no place in court decisions, but as a lawyer and thanks to her husband, a prosecutor, with whom she does not live, she was able to win the favor of the judges who gave her a place of choice: she was able to obtain open visits with Thimeo very quickly and this since his placement by the ASE. I still can't understand how, given her emotional closeness to Julio and geographical closeness to my son's aggressor (she always lived above Michelle and Melissa!), the judge was able to give her such an important role with Thimeo.

My parents tell me that my son will not be fooled for long by her schemes. According to them, he is not so attached to her but he is happy to go to his Corsican village because he has found friends there with whom he gets along well.

Thimeo is unaware of what this woman has been and still is with her father. He doesn't know the trust I had in her and the disappointments she caused me, hastening my downfall a little more. She, who never wanted to be a mother, has taken over my son, who is also Julio's son, and I am sure that this is the main reason why she takes care of him in this way: to keep a special place in the Corsican family.

Chapter 17
Do as I say, but don't do as I do

Summer 2015, barely gone, so I returned to Paris after five days.

When I arrived, I had to face my father's contemptuous look and my mother's pained look... As my father didn't want to keep me, he called Chris, my half-brother who lives in Sète, to find me a cure in the region. And in the meantime: no medication, no alcohol...

And here I am with my father in the middle of a withdrawal crisis on the way to Sète! We arrived late at the station and as soon as we sat down at my brother's table, my father said to me: "I'm sorry: if you can't drink anymore, I can, and I have such a sore throat...". I was sitting in front of him, discomfited, pale and really in withdrawal. Supposedly to soothe his sore throat, he asked my brother for a whiskey... My God! I can still smell it! I could see myself getting up, snatching the glass from his hands and drinking it so much I wanted to! I wanted to throw it all away, to scream, I found the ordeal unacceptable... So I went out promising them that I wouldn't go far. My goal was of course to find something to drink and I think I found a flask or two at a grocery store. I wandered around and then went home. I was thinking about Thimeo, at that woman's house I felt miserable. I had nothing to hold on to.

The next day we drove more than an hour and a half to the center... We went in and when Chris saw the weirdos there he said to me: "Gigi, we're not leaving you here..."

Dad approved, we got my stuff and left. So we stayed only three days in Sète. I admit I was relieved, even though I knew it wasn't a solution... I drank less, but I still drank. A little wine here and a drink there .... I took everything that came along, I didn't miss any opportunity...

I also remember one time when I was still in terrible need of alcohol and my father had to accompany me somewhere. I don't remember where because of the alcohol, I always have memory lapses... We were both in the car and as my father was hungry we stopped in a restaurant... where he ordered a bottle of wine! I couldn't take it anymore. While he was drinking, I hardly ate anything, I went out for a smoke several times, and to top it all off, he asked the waiter to leave with the bottle of wine under his arm! Like a suffering multiplied, the incomprehension of my father hurt me so much... In addition to the lack, I struggled not to faint.

My father is seventy-nine years old and I know that for him alcohol is inseparable from food. If he doesn't drink, he sulks and eats nothing. He too is an alcoholic, but he doesn't realize it. And even though he has seen me suffer, he has never spared me.

For example, for Christmas 2018, when I wasn't drinking at all (and now I was definitely sober), he asked me to stop and get twenty-four bottles of wine for the holidays... It's like asking someone who has stopped shooting up to bring drugs for others... It seems to me that my father could have been a little more tactful. It seemed like he didn't remember what I went through, which he did witness...

But it must be said that for a parent to see his child destroying himself, or even helping him to drink so that he doesn't get worse, there is nothing worse... To see his child become another, the suffering, the anger, the feeling of powerlessness, when there is so much love between us. It must have been terrible for them... That's also why I find it hard to understand my father.

But I forgive his lack of knowledge of the disease that also made him suffer a lot. I hope that they will forgive me too, even if it is especially the forgiveness of my son that counts in my eyes.

I would also like to say that it suits many people to have an alcoholic in their family. It allows them to not think about their own situation. And then with an alcoholic time passes quickly, you have to take care of him, go to the doctors, discuss to try to end this situation.

CHAPTER 18
MY SON AND THE ESA

September 2015; for the start of the school year Thimeo let all the pain in his heart explode and the whole family was destroyed.

We were at my parents' house. I hadn't had a drink in two days, I had seen my mom's shrink or a doctor and I was on medication.

That morning I tried to wake Thimeo up but he was not well, he did not want to get up. To force him to go to school, my father and my cousin Thomas pulled him out of bed violently, dragging him by his feet to the floor. My son, who was crying his heart out, hung out the window... He had a real nervous breakdown. I tried to talk to him, to console him, I took him in my arms and we went in the garden... We made a hug but his heart remained sad and by seeing his distress I took the decision to call the firemen, whom I imagined to be in empathy, because my father did not deny it, it was necessary that he went to the school whereas the anger and the sadness of Thimeo continued more and more.

The firemen saw him and took him to the Antoine-Béclère hospital where the ASE intervened. They kept him in the hospital for ten days. Without anyone realizing it, the machine was on its way: they were taking my son away from me. He became a child placed by the ASE in a foster family, in Dourdan. This should normally be done after an interview with the mother, but I was not entitled to it, because according to them my son had attempted to defenestrate... While he had simply clung to what he could to resist my father and my cousin.

During the ten days that Thimeo was in the hospital, they obviously made him talk and my son couldn't hide that I was drinking, that I was relapsing, that we were mostly at my parents' house and that he didn't want to go to our apartment anymore, or to this school...

My mother and I went to the hospital every day to see him and bring him things... Then we were told that we should not come anymore: an order from the TGI of Nanterre was immediately pronounced for a placement in a foster home.

What a waste! I hope so much that he will be able to recover from the traumas that I and then the ASE put him through, and that he will not hold a grudge against me for the rest of his life. I hope that there is a part of his heart that will understand my distress and that he will forgive me, that he will understand a little what I went through to get there. And that if he can never forgive me, at least that he can give himself the means to have a happy and fulfilled life. Unfortunately, I know that this is not the case at the moment.

So Thimeo was placed from September 2015 to May 2017, in this foster family in Dourdan in Essonne. We were only allowed to see each other once a month in a mediated visit: first one hour, then after some time we were allowed two hours together... And how quickly it goes by! Just enough time to hug him, give him some things, ask him how he is... But can we really share and find each other when there are two ladies scrutinizing your every move, interpreting your every word? I was worried and curious, but I could see that Thimeo could not talk to me freely about what he was experiencing there. The ASE considered that he was in a "perfect" family, when in reality his daily life was not easy. No contact was allowed with the foster family. My father went there anyway to see Thimeo, to see these strangers and to know if his grandson was with good people... Of course, the ASE reproached him for this burst of concern and love...

I, who was forbidden to see my son, took advantage of the appointments fixed by his school to go there earlier and thus be able to hug him for a few seconds. It displeased Mrs. Minime, the "mother" of the foster family, to see that I could be there and steal a few seconds with my son. I never felt any kindness, compassion or heard a kind word from her... But my son was happy to see me and that was the main thing.

Thimeo was placed, but in the reports of the ASE filed with the Court of Nanterre, at no time is it stated that he was an abused child, neglected, without affection or that I failed in his education. He is described as an intelligent child, with a lot of intellectual capacities, sociable. It is true that I was an alcoholic, but one does not place a child who is surrounded by a caring family, who is concerned about his well-being, who goes to school and who is followed by psychologists. All this without taking into account the past that Thimeo and I had.

This situation drove me even deeper into alcohol. Why didn't the judge tell me, "Ma'am, go to six months of treatment and we'll give you your son back"? It's a system that doesn't have the means of its ambitions and that has plunged Thimeo into a certain "institutional abuse", to use the words of one of our educators.

Since I was not allowed to see him I wrote to him, sent him packages with surprises inside. I was able to read afterwards, in the reports of the ASE, that I wrote to my son as I would to "a lover"... I was literally disgusted to see this. I was encouraged to write to him to turn this against me! I was criticized for not working, but the appointments that the ESA gave me could fall on any day, always during the day. What employer would accept to see his employee leave for an afternoon here, a morning there? And my son was in the same situation, he often had to miss school.

The ASE does not really take into consideration the well-being of the child, because the well-being of the parents is also part of the child's well-being and I was not treated well. The ladies I met were always judgmental, they didn't take into account everything I had to endure during Thimeo's childhood to protect him. They would not give me any credit, they even tried to rewrite our history with their own interpretation... What right did they have to do that?

Especially since if I never missed an appointment, I knew that this was not the case for Julio, who either didn't come or left before the end of the appointment, leaving his son in great sadness.

And Thimeo's daily life was no fun, he was placed in this family with two other children. The parents of the older one were drug addicts and abusers and the other little girl, whose parent had committed suicide, kept bothering Thimeo with a heavy story as well... He was never at peace because he was made to go back and forth regularly, either to see me (once a month), or to see his father, my parents, my brother, his godmother Camilla... Not to mention the appointments he had with these two ladies, alone, without the family.

It was non-stop for him. This rhythm could only disturb his schooling. Especially since these appointments only stirred up the past, without building a possible future within his family. The past, the surveillance, the lies, a falsification of the truth, and their influence on a young child against his family: this cannot give positive appointments to move forward. And I don't dare to think about the brainwashing he must have faced when he was constantly asked to tell his story.

I had made a request for him to be followed by a psychologist or in a CMP (medical-psychological center), but these ladies never answered favorably under the pretext that the foster family did not have the time to accompany him, in addition to what she already had to do.

In 2016 Thimeo returned to college and I was not allowed to attend his first day of school either. Of course, because the appointment schedule didn't change, he had to keep making up classes. He was not like the other children in this school and the ASE started to tell me that Thimeo was becoming violent at school, fighting, insulting the foster family.

As for me, I looked forward to my appointments with my son, I continued to drink but never when I went to see him. I was very careful to look good, even though I knew he could see in my face that I hadn't stopped. I still wanted the appointments to go as smoothly as possible since we saw each other so little. The ESA, after telling me all these things about my son, in front of him, expected me to re-frame it. While she had taken away all my prerogatives as a mother, she seemed to make me responsible for my son's education and rhythm of life, which I had not chosen. I was trying to understand his malaise. I would have liked to be more present for Thimeo but in this situation what could I do? I was not with him, I was not aware of the problems he was going through. They were the ones responsible for his change in behavior and actions. I was getting more and more worried and drinking more between appointments.

I was still living with my parents, but the addictologist tried to reassure me by telling me that he had known a woman who was even more alcoholic than I was who had managed to get her children back. He also told me that this system was a system that broke, crushed the children and the family. And I could see that my son was being prepared for our meetings, because it was Thimeo who was asking me when I was going to go back to work, he was the one asking me questions and talking to me about the "psychological work" that we had to do together. The words of the ASE came out of my son's mouth... Wouldn't the role of the ASE and the judge have been on the contrary to help me so that Thimeo could find his family, his mother? I guess not.

I was a shadow of my former self.

I was no longer a happy mother who loves and protects her child for a long time.

I wasn't even a mother anymore because my child had been taken away from me.

One day, I learned that Thimeo had missed the evening bus after school. He had to cross the forest of Dourdan alone to reach the village where he lived because the mother of the foster family could not come to pick him up and the father did not want to interfere with the children who were under the responsibility of his wife.

My sadness was so great to imagine my child alone in that wood that I could do nothing but drink, to ease the pain, to forget... My reason to live was being taken away, and I drank to feel stronger. I just wanted to heal my pain, but in reality I was drowning myself and my grief with my best friend, alcohol.

I didn't have my son anymore. The heartbreak is indescribable. I was screaming with pain inside.

Except for when I had to see the ladies from the ESA or the one hour a month when I could finally see my son, the rest of the time was spent looking for alcohol. I took the car, I changed grocery stores, I alternated, I went to the store... In front of my parents I used the excuse of walking the dog and I continued to hide the flasks in my pants, my socks, in my big boots, in my bag. The scenario was always the same: I would drink one in the street on the way home and hide it in a bush. When we cleaned up, we found empty bottles everywhere in closets, gloves, hoods, pockets, bags, behind papers... You can't imagine the energy you spend to find and hide alcohol... Not to mention that I drank my father's wine, who even had to put a lock on the cellar and the fridge... It was no good at all...

One day the ladies from the ASE encouraged me to file a complaint following the result of the juvenile brigade. Even if it was going to stir up everything again, I had to close, turn this page for Thimeo and me... So that's what I did, I filed a civil suit for my son and myself... Once I had made my decision, I came up against my parents, my brother, who thought that I was going to "stir up shit" again and that we didn't need this.

Yet, even though it took time, it was perhaps the best advice these ladies gave me... I was still far from quitting alcohol, though. Instead, it was pulling me back into the files, the photocopies, the certifications, the hell of it all.

To reassure myself, I thought that it might do Thimeo good to be away from the family for a while and because of their smooth talk, I had no idea what he was going through and what his father was doing to him in terms of disappointment for not coming or cutting the appointments short. I had no idea what Thimeo was going through. He couldn't confide in me, we were never alone. And the time passed.

Later Thimeo ended up running away and phoning my father to come and get him. Since 2017 my son has been living with his grandparents, with an AEMO (Aide à l'Education en milieu ouvert). We slowly got closer in 2018, at Christmas time, but he remains very angry at me and blames me for ruining his life. He currently refuses to see me again. Obviously he will never forgive me for not having had a childhood like others because of my alcoholism.

I left a child and I am faced with a teenager who is not doing well.... And even though I have parental authority,

I can't do anything. You can't force your son to see you if he doesn't want to... We'll meet at his own pace, I'm there for him. Now that I'm sober to the core, I'm trying to save him, to help him, to help my parents to take steps...

But before I got to that point, years went by where alcohol remained deeply embedded in my metabolism.

Chapter 19
Against a backdrop of alcohol, the meeting!!!

Summer 2016. Thimeo had been placed for almost a year.

For the vacations, in my state of great alcoholic assumed, I followed my parents on the island of Ré. I would never have had the pretention, me who was going further and further in the destruction of myself, to make this unimaginable dream... To make the Meeting which was going to save my life !!!

In the meantime, the car ride was horrible because I was craving alcohol and my whole body was suffering. As you can see, when I was with my mother I could drink a little, but in the presence of my father it was out of the question, so there was no antidote to the pain. The air conditioning hurt my head, I grumbled, my hands were sweaty, I couldn't stand for long... My parents didn't realize how bad my withdrawal was, they even went to a highway restaurant and didn't bring me back a beer... Non-alcoholics have no idea what it feels like to be in physical withdrawal from alcohol. I waited for them, one step away from going to the truckers parked next door. The only reason I didn't was because I could barely stand.

When we arrived at the campsite, my first instinct was to find out where the restaurant/bar was. And the man who would become the man of my life was working there.

So I arrived, with my big hat and dark glasses, and after saying hello I asked to buy a bottle of whiskey. I didn't want just a drink, I was in withdrawal, I needed alcohol - a bottle, and there was no vodka. The owner of the campsite restaurant was in the back room and so I had to deal with the waiter... It was like a flash, this handsome man with his long and silky hair, his natural elegance, his devastating smile, and above all he was immediately kind and attentive to me.

We introduced ourselves. His name was Clément, and I said to him, not haughty but sure of myself: "I am a journalist, I am an alcoholic, I want a bottle and I have the right, I am of age and I will be a good customer..."

It made him laugh... but gently, not mockingly...

So Clement knew right away that I was a big drinker. He went to his boss and I ended up getting my bottle. I felt happy, because I knew I had made a great encounter and that I was going to end the physical pain of withdrawal with the first sip.

And indeed, as soon as I had my bottle, I went to drink it in the camping's toilets. Immediately, I felt much better, my hands were no longer clammy, I had no more headache, in short I was alive again. I hid the bottle in my bag and went back to the bungalow, in a good mood, to find my parents who didn't suspect anything. During the meal at the restaurant I even dared to order a martini in front of my father. He wasn't happy about it, but that's how it was; he didn't mind drinking in front of me!

Thimeo was in different host families, since his was on vacation. We didn't have any contact and I suffered a lot. I saw the children in the campsite, and I had to get over that pain too. Drinking was, again, the way to cope with the laughter, the visions of children who were happy with their family, on vacation. I was in an abyss, but I wanted to enjoy my vacation too and find a little bit of carefree spirit, which would be the case thanks to my meeting with Clément.

As a waiter he had free time and he juggled perfectly... I was amazed by his zest for life, his good mood, his humor... I would join him when he was on break and he would teach me to juggle, but I was so drunk that I would fall. It was funny. Pitiful but funny. I was making fun of myself. One night we met at the beach next to the campground. He had come with some beers and I told him everything. I told him my life in great detail and in no uncertain terms: that I had a son, that he was in care, that I was an alcoholic since Thimeo had been the victim of incest. I also told him about my professional life before... My frankness and my charm made him fall in love with me, we kissed and we were not going to leave each other anymore.

Soon my days were set to his schedule. During his breaks, he would go to the supermarket and bring me back bottles of vodka, a few beers that he kept in the fridge of his caravan. We talked a lot and cuddled, we went for a walk on the shore. When he was working, I would wait for him in his caravan, which I would tidy up, or I would lie down and listen to music and we knew we were experiencing something strong.

Meeting Clement is important because it is "thanks" to him that I am still alive and sober today... I think I would have died if I had not known him.

When I met Clement, he didn't suspect this real physical and psychological need because I was a happy drunk: I was laughing, I was funny, alive, in love with him. Then I had a destructive side in our relationship, drinking more and more, with time and trials. I was dark and sad.... He didn't expect that when we met. I was going to give him a hard time, but neither he nor I knew that yet. And thanks to him, to his love and perseverance, I was going to get out of alcohol... In the meantime, we simply tasted the happiness of being together and he understood me, understood my story, my path, my suffering and my sorrows... The bar owner had told him that I would never get out of it. And I proved him right for two years. Clément often told me about this anecdote. But the boss was wrong, I finally got out of it. I proved everyone wrong! Clément has always believed in me and I am proud of him, that he has held on... That is a true proof of Love...

When we met, my friend already knew the ravages of alcohol, because his parents had run a bar. So he'd known a lot of losers, but not ones like me. His father immediately put people in their place. Clement thought I was an alcoholic out of desperation, for a period of time, but not in withdrawal to that extent. He didn't know about the alcoholic disease.

One day my father arrived at the caravan, saying aloud to Clément, "I hope you didn't fuck my daughter"... Too late! And on top of that we loved each other! My father almost dragged me on the floor to our mobile home. He must have been drinking too and thought I wasn't behaving like a good girl. He thought Clement was a vacation sweetheart, but it was more than that, I knew. A little later Clément met my mother who saw that he was kind to me.

I drank so much that my father hid bottles of wine in the bushes next to our place, which he brought out just as we were about to eat... Then he forced me to stay in the mobile home. As a result, I was so desperate that I called the nearest doctor. He received me very quickly, and gave me a shot of Valium... What a relief! Immediately I felt better. Afterwards, we went back to the campsite with my father, but even with the medication I continued to drink with Clément... and in the mobile home, I was sleeping. One day when I was not well because I had drunk too much, my parents called the doctor who had me hospitalized for three days in La Rochelle, I had a high blood alcohol level...

On my way out I found my friend Clément in good shape. I had a treatment but I continued to drink slowly. Then my parents realized that my man was truly benevolent and at the end of our vacation I was able to spend the nights in his caravan. My parents got used to it, and since I drank a little but not too much, I was doing pretty well.

Our vacations finished, we did not imagine ourselves far from each other... The morning of our departure, with the agreement of my parents, Clément sneaked out to follow me, while the season was not finished. We went back to the Nièvre, to my parents' country house.

Happiness at last! I hadn't been this happy in a long time! I felt loved for myself and accepted despite and with my heavy past and the alcoholic situation I was in. On the way back, we stopped at a small bistro for lunch on the terrace. When everyone was at the table, I pretended to go to the toilet to ask for a triple whisky and coke which I paid for immediately, asking the manager not to say anything...

One of the tricks of the alcoholic is to drink on the sly. You become very good at this game, you never miss an opportunity.

Of course I went back a second time before the end of the meal. No one noticed or suspected.

We stayed a few days in the Nièvre, but my father drank, and so did we. We hid the beers that allowed us to decompress. When I went shopping with my mother, I would go on my own and buy flasks of vodka that I drank from the parking lot and hid in my bag. It was obvious that I was cheating, that I was drunk... So my friend decided that we would go and join his mother in the Yonne, to get me off drugs and away from my family, to break my drinking habits.

When we left, my father had to accompany us to the station. Sitting in the car, my mother put a pill in my mouth that turned my head... I started to feel the effects on the train and when we had to walk across Sens, I was a real vegetable. We finally arrived at Clément's mother's house, who welcomed me with open arms. We didn't stay very long, because I drank beer, cider and a little wine, but it wasn't enough. As I still had some medicine left, I made bad mixtures, and sometimes I got angry, or sad...

Clément then proposed me to go to the grape harvest... I knew that it was going to be hard and I was a little bit afraid but we went to get my car which was at my parents' in Paris and we went there.

It was royal, we were very well received, Clément had received the plan from a friend of his who owned a wine bar in Paris. We were several grape pickers and we were there to make quality. The premises were beautiful, there was a drum set, a table soccer, alcohol flowed freely with a beer dispenser.

The important thing was that we worked well. I was allowed to drink a little but not to get high. We would get up early in the morning and cut the grapes, separating the ripe from the rotten ones. We had to be careful not to crush the bunches. At ten o'clock we had a break, with pate, snacks and wine as much as we wanted, but in the morning we drank water and went back to work until noon.

The meals were prepared by a caterer and on the table there were bottles of wine from the estate. We drank sensibly, because harvesting is extremely tiring and the slopes of the vineyards were steep. At the four o'clock break, there was also food and drink. Either we had a glass of wine or a beer... and then the evening came. We would quickly go to the shower, then to the beer tap. While waiting for everyone to be ready for dinner, everyone would drink... Then, when dinner was over, we would play backgammon, drink again but slowly and go to bed early because we knew that the next day was going to be hard...

I was able to keep up the pace for all ten days, which was not easy at first. I did it by being able to cut out the drugs and drink less alcohol.

The only downside was that I had to miss an appointment with ESA and Thimeo to do this work. My son blamed me a lot for this, as did the ladies at the ASE, telling me that I had no right to not comply with the schedule, whatever the reason. So I was blamed for not working and when I did work I was not allowed to miss an appointment.

It made me feel guilty. And then I got better, I had relearned how to exercise, I had stopped taking medication, I had regained a normal weight and height... For an alcoholic, getting cured by going to the grape harvest is a bit incongruous but it worked. I was healthy again, with an obvious weight loss due to the cessation of medication. I wasn't taking any medication at all... What a victory!!!

It was also during this harvest, on September 2, 2016, that the court decision recognizing Thimeo as a victim of incest was rendered by the Council Chamber of the Paris Children's Court, declaring that Melissa was found guilty of the facts she was accused of, that she should have judicial protection until she came of age; condemning Melissa's civilly responsible parents and giving Thimeo and myself damages.

I might as well say that it was not a sum worthy of what we had suffered: 2000 euros for Thimeo and 1160 for me... This did not even cover the legal fees incurred, but the judgment was rendered and no one could say anymore that what Thimeo had endured was a lie...

Yet ALL the damage had already been done: the psychological abuse of the father and his family, the atrocious scenes we had lived through, the procedures for alimony that remained unanswered, the painful procedures, the alcoholism, the ASE... It's the obstacle course when you are a victim. We don't say it enough. I blame the Justice system even if in the end "justice was done"... but at what price, and after how long? What remains is the ASE and alcohol, the broken and shattered lives.

In October 2016, with Clement we tried to move to Paris, to the apartment where I had lived with Julio during my pregnancy and in which I had experienced great moments of disillusionment, alone with my son during his first year. Overwhelmed by these memories, and with the neighborhood having stores everywhere, I fell back in. I couldn't stop myself from drinking in secret, even if it was obvious that I was drinking... I ruined the wedding of Clément's best friend, the one who had found us the harvest plan, because I was in no condition, I couldn't stand it anymore... He still holds a grudge against me and besides, they still don't speak to each other with his friend...

Paris... There was the noise, too many people, too many stores... The past was too heavy to carry. Anyway my Clément was beginning to understand : I had to get away from all these memories, good or bad...

He would sometimes make sure to drink as much as I did so that I would realize what state I was in. But it ended up in an argument. So one day we left without thinking with my car, after writing on the walls: *freedom !!!!!,* and other horrors, some of which were a bit insulting to my mother, my parents.

What people don't know is how much I would still be mad at myself for everything I did, and at each of them, but that anger needed to come out.

Last night, we were talking about the book I am writing with Clement and some anecdotes I was recounting... My friend told me something that I think is important: not to be too hard on myself because there have been times when I have had a lot less alcohol and better management... He pointed out that it was always on the eve of or following events, bad news that I would binge, but that I had also tried to stop drinking several times.

Still, I did a lot of damage to my son by disappointing him... I caused him a lot of emotional pain. And I will always blame myself... You can't fix that, and I don't know if you can forgive it.

So Justice... For me who always believed in it, even if it was finally rendered, it was only pain and suffering. So much time spent until exhaustion to constitute the files and that was my loss. My son obtained "justice" but at what price? He lost his mother, and his childhood... maybe his future...

CHAPTER 20
DRINKING IN THE CAMPER

So at the end of October 2016 we went back to Clément's mom's house in this little village next to Sens...

I continued to drink: cider, liqueurs, beers and vodka. The friends from the village would come by and it was always a chance to have a drink, but we had established a ritual with Clément: every day we would go for a walk in the forest. We took two beers with us to take a break, but we walked well and we saw deer, nature ... We left the house and we breathed...

Unfortunately, I did some more of my own there. The bad alcohol was taking over and I couldn't control myself even though we were at Clement's mother's house. He was pushing me to react but I was not able to.

We were looking for a way to be independent, to get away from my worries and to be able to move around and work together without being tied to one place. Without being gypsies or caravans, Clément's whole family started to make a living by working in a mobile way with caravans. He himself was born in his parents' caravan... before they settled in this small village in the Yonne. His mother, in addition to the restaurant, was a canteen worker and his father ran the bar. He too had become an alcoholic, so Clément saw him mistreating his mother. Not having had a happy childhood, my friend never wanted to have children. This made him very hard on his personality. As soon as he turned 17, Clement left home and was always traveling... He lived in London for 14 years, then in Greece, Amsterdam, Berlin...

As he was always talking about freedom and his experience, we naturally moved to a motor home. Anyway, without my son, I couldn't see myself living anywhere, I was lost, broken, shattered... I only knew that I had one appointment per month for which I had to return to Paris, to see Thimeo. A rhythm that leaves no respite to rebuild.

Once the camper was bought, in my name because Clément didn't have the license, we headed for the sea and Port-Saint-Louis. We stopped on the way, drinking a little in the evening, and then we took the road again.

Once we arrived, we refilled our water supplies every two days in the cemeteries. But hardly the time to breathe a little and it was already necessary to think of going back to Paris for my appointment with Thimeo and these ladies who asked me what I was doing. Obviously, the fact of traveling and having a camper van, maybe to work, did not reassure anyone. If it was convenient for my parents because they didn't have me under their responsibility anymore, they also found it unstable and hoped that it wouldn't last too long...

We were on the road for a year and a half. Anxiety and stress never left me. Just like alcohol, they were my two new friends. Clement was there, but in my heart it was a constant battle. I was at my lowest point, but I was driving during the day. The more I was suffering inside for my son at the ASE, the more I drank in the evening, and the more I hurt Clément who was only looking for beautiful places for us to live the moment and make beautiful memories... For me it was the opposite, my preoccupations veiled all that. Alcohol was stealing these moments from me, from both of us.

Every month, we had to come back to Plessis-Robinson for the appointments with my Thimeo and the ASE. I was allowed to have a few free visits with my son and I took the opportunity to take him in the camper and introduce him to Clément, whom he had heard a lot about during my previous visits.

I wanted to reassure him that we had a life that was acceptable until we found a place to settle down. We had a great time and I heard Thimeo's laughter when Clement did magic tricks for him. It had been so long! Then the three of us had a snack and at the appointed time, I walked Thimeo back to the ESA. I thought we had spent those two hours beautifully, it was a happy moment: I had heard my son's laughter, I had had him close to me.

But afterwards the ASE reproached me for this visit by telling me that Thimeo would have preferred to spend the day alone with me, that he had not been happy to come in the camper... He was however dead of laughter and well installed in the nasturtium to look at the lights of all the colors that we had installed with Clément. Who had put these ideas in his head? It seems obvious to me that the ASE is rewriting history as they see fit, and we can't say anything.

Between each meeting we went back on the road with Clément...

In the camper we discussed about everything and nothing, then we watched TV on our smartphones, we tried to drink while eating but the evening arrived and with it the stress to miss alcohol. We would then go to look for a bottle or two in order to spend the evening. We drank by taking the aperitif but while Clément was under the shower I refilled me and put water in the bottle of wine. Of course he noticed and it made him furious. He told me that every time I drank on the sly, it was like cheating on him with another man, that it had the same effect on him.

When we came back to Le Plessis, we would park next to a park ten minutes walk from the ASE. We had come from all over France, I was exhausted and still sick from alcohol. Tired, I drank the night before the appointment to decompress, both from the road and from the next day's appointment. I was anxious because I never knew what these ladies were going to tell me about my son and how the appointment was going to go. Thimeo was becoming violent and aggressive at school and they expected me to react, to lecture him. They were analyzing everything but I had the legitimate impression that none of my reactions were going to be the right one... I had very few elements finally; it was especially the expression of Thimeo's uneasiness and the fact that the framework in which he grew up did not suit him.

After the reflection on the presence of Clément, I received Thimeo alone in the camper... Once I went to pick him up at the ASE for a new free outing. Thimeo had asked me to buy him a phone, I had ordered it, but it had not yet arrived. My son started to cry and was hard to console. The appointment was not starting well. When I asked him if he had eaten, he said he had not. Of course I made him something to eat, but I told myself that if the ESA ladies had wanted it to go wrong, they wouldn't have done it any other way.

Thimeo told me very little about what he was doing, what he was going through... He didn't want to worry me and the appointments were short. I would have a lot to say about this system.

After each meeting we left with Clément, but then the free outings were taken away from me, because I did not bring enough stability to Thimeo... However the camper van avoided us to take the transport, and to go where besides? In an impersonal café, without intimacy? We did not have time to go to Paris in two hours nor to go to the cinema. For all these reasons, the camper was a good solution.

With Clément, we went to Nantes in May to do the lily of the valley. I was willing but still in alcohol. We did one day of work and we left early the next day because I had gone crazy. My worries with Thimeo did not leave my mind.

One day, at the ASE, Thimeo arrived in a wet T-shirt. That day it was pouring rain. He was without a jacket, wet to the skin, I had to take him to the bathroom to wipe him off and give him one of my sweaters... However, at no time did the ladies at the ASE give the foster family a second thought, as if this were normal.

As the appointments with the people from the ASE were sometimes multiple, and always on dates that suited them, with Clément we were looking for places to park not too far from Paris - close to cemeteries to have a watering hole and quiet to spend some time there. The appointments with the ASE at this rate were driving me crazy. I was asked to be stable but I was sure I didn't want to live in Paris again.

With these appointments once or several times a month, I couldn't move far away, go abroad, Thimeo and the ASE would have taken it as an abandonment... And what employer would accept to hire someone who has so many appointments and must travel so much? How can you be stable? The pressure was constant! And the solutions were non-existent.

I used to take out my anger and frustration on Clément. As the camper was in my name, I don't know how many times I dared to chase him away from "my home", even though it was our common life project, "the good intermediate solution" that we had found together. But I did not accept the social decline that I was experiencing, and that Thimeo, that the ASE made me feel.

I threw Clément's things out of the door dozens of times, I shouted, I screamed, I threw everything, I spilled everything. I rejected the one who still loved me and who despite everything stayed with me... I called him an "asshole" when I was the asshole. I hurt him so much. His bag was always ready, he was constantly insecure.

We spent in the camper some good times, but mostly a lot of bad ones. He smelled of alcohol, I smelled of alcohol, I sweated alcohol at night... It was endless. All those fights inside! And then it would calm down, I would drink, we would drink, we would have sex... It's kind of strange to know that you're almost part of a tribe of people who have chosen to live outside of society by not having a permanent home. I felt very *insecure*. I felt that this life was not for me. I couldn't get used to the idea. The proof was that everywhere we went, I was drinking once we got there. We spent nights and days in supermarket parking lots where I got drunk. When we chose beautiful and bucolic places, I always spoiled everything with my alcohol.

One day when we were in Orleans, we went for a walk and then to a bar. I was talking to everyone. Clément with his protective instinct, and his foresighted mistrust, didn't drink as much as I did and was a little out of the way. I then went out to smoke, and I don't remember what I said, but we found ourselves surrounded by five or six boys, also drunk, who were telling Clément "that when you have a bitch of a wife like me, you have to keep her tied up. That almost turned very badly... We left quickly by taking care not to be followed but we were close to an explosive and dangerous fight because of me.

Chapter 21
Alcoholic Madness

With time, I understood that it is a very bad idea to drink to forget or when you feel sad, simply because alcohol is the best anxiolytic in the world. That's how you can fall into alcoholism. Alcohol should be saved for joyful and exceptional moments. There is no such thing as drinking when you're feeling bad to get better. It is an illusion that can cost you and your loved ones dearly.

Alcohol can make you cry, it can make you happy, but I had gone so far that, after a few drinks, I was no longer happy or sad... I expressed an anger of frustration, pain and suffering and it was explosive. In these cases, I become mean in my words, provocative, aggressive, I break everything, I fall on the floor, I shout, I throw out the door all the objects I find even if they mean something to me, and I always manage to drink more when there is some, and if not I go back to look for more while staggering. And I find some! And then I drink, I drink more and faster, and then I fall. Or I spend my time begging my friend to get me a bottle of alcohol for fear of the withdrawal that might hit me, or I sleep... But in reality it often ends up in the hospital.

The cravings, the "*craving*" as the doctors say, are, I think, the most excruciating thing. You have sweaty hands, your heart is going a hundred times an hour, you can't stand up but you can't lie still, you're squirming, you have a terrible feeling of anxiety, your hands are shaking, you can't even light a cigarette, your head hurts and you're almost unable to speak, you just have the strength to shout "give me some alcohol!" And then, if you are given some, from the first big sip, it is immediately better... All these symptoms disappear, you become a normal person again... Even if it stings, this first sip! And that it is hot when the alcohol is strong... But what an immediate relief! It is very impressive.

To avoid this, my friend would sometimes reluctantly get me a bottle. He would call my mom to find out what to do... In my quieter moments I would go to a doctor to get some medicine. What is really dangerous is mixing alcohol and medication, we know where that leads: to the morgue buddy... And how many of us alcoholics have done it? All of us!!!

Fortunately, I was lucky enough to get through it because I was a little bit careful, I alternated between taking alcohol and medication.

In April 2017 we stopped in Saché, we were by the water in this charming little village and there was a grocery store. Clement didn't agree, but I went to get some alcohol and drank on the way back.

Clément had preferred to take the air and I took the opportunity to go back for alcohol. That's when I had a fit of alcoholic dementia.

A little further on there was a group of young people having a barbecue, and I turned up the heat all by myself, ripped out all the wires from the camper's battery. Clement came back and I blocked all the doors. He punched the vehicle while I kicked the door and broke it.

The guys who were there threatened to kill us if we didn't leave. It was very tense, everyone was shouting very loudly. Clement magically managed to reconnect some wires quickly and we were able to leave, both of us scared to death. I don't remember where we stopped, but I know that I was badly argued and that the wires of the camper van caused us a lot of problems afterwards.

It's the same scenario every time. After the drinking, I notice the material damage; the next day I look at the cigarette holes in the clothes, on the sofas, the bed, the lost or broken things. And then I discover the damage on myself: bruises everywhere, a dirty face, blisters, burns on hands, legs, even face... And I don't talk about the hateful things I might have said under the influence of alcohol.

Because I was drinking so much, I couldn't go to the bathroom alone. Clément had to carry me. I didn't care what people thought of me anymore, even if it meant putting myself in danger.

I still managed to find enough energy to go and get some alcohol and nobody minded. I was staggering, but nobody, neither the people I passed, nor the salesmen or the grocers never made a remark to me... To give me strength I put the bottle in my scarf and I drank some sips... I wasn't waiting to get home, I was craving.

And as it is true that violence calls for violence, I received some slaps, fruit of the confusion of my friend. Under the effect of alcohol, you can't feel anything, so I kept throwing things out the door and threatening him. How many times did I call the police? More than once for assault and battery... Clement actually spent the night in the gnouf on the evening of December 24, 2017 in Bagneux.

Despite everything I put him through, he was there, and he still is. That is the most beautiful proof of love you can give to someone. To love in spite of the disease.

He was desperate for me not to change. He tried to talk to me about my son, but that only made me more demoralized. He talked to me about our future. But what future? To leave, to leave my son, to go where? I was crushed by my problems and the only way to forget was to drink. The past and the present are sometimes so heavy that you can't think about the future... This is the typical pattern of an alcoholic: the destruction of everything and everyone, those around you and yourself.

It's obvious, I know it: when I drink, I have no love for myself and no love for those who love me. There is no more love for myself, no more limits. I know I'm hurting myself by drinking but I do it anyway... My son rejected me, my parents got angry and unloaded on my friend who didn't know what to do... Obviously, it had to come from me... That I had to *click*... But in reality, we look for the *trigger* at the bottom of the bottle.

I've heard: "Oh it's easy for you alcoholics, you make a mess and then you don't remember anything the next day!" as if the realization of what you've thrown away, destroyed, the guilt you already feel, the wounds in your soul weren't deep enough.

Chapter 22
Failed Escape at Nemours

On May 4, 2017, we stopped in Nemours at the waterfront. We stayed there because I was waiting for the next appointment with ESA and we didn't want to go back and forth under these circumstances.

We thought we would stay for a week, the time for Clément to find out about his driver's license. I held on long enough for him to start his registration and do his evaluation. On my side I continued to drink, only in the evening but I was looking forward to these moments... And then, during a walk, I took the opportunity to buy some vodka and there was no more question of limits.

One day I drank so much that my friend called my mother to ask if he should buy me more alcohol. My parents told him no: "Now that's enough... Never mind the consequences..." So I started to break everything and my friend called the fire department in the afternoon.

I ended up in the hospital in a semi-conscious state. I was tied up by my feet and chest. When I said I wanted to go to the bathroom they put a urinary catheter in me: it hurts and to pee you have to press with your hands on the bladder. I felt that it was going to pass but with the pain it blocks everything, it's not natural.

After a while they untied me. I had my clothes on, not my bag, but I didn't care, still drunk as I was. So I tried to leave and the nurses at the hospital immediately called security. I didn't have a chance, but I kept going and managed to get to the entrance of the hospital... They dragged me to the floor, but I ran away again and went to hide behind a car in the parking lot. There a nurse came, who spoke to me kindly and made me understand that I had no choice but to follow him, either with the soft way, by myself, or it would be the hard way....

I followed him and they reattached me, completely this time, strapped me in up to my neck. It wasn't the first time, I knew how it worked, the noises, the smells, the comings and goings of the hospital staff, the patients looking at you. It traumatizes little by little, unconsciously, the emotional shock is there. I was shocked by the image I was sending back of myself in this situation but it was proportional to my pain, so I accepted it.

I spent the night in the hospital and was released the next day. Twenty-four hours without smoking or being able to move... I called Clement who was coming to join me. I wasn't well. They let you out of the hospital but they don't give you any medicine to get better, so all you can think about is drinking again, but when you're not alone you can't, so you suffer from the inside: headaches, tremors, general weakness... And then the shame, not only towards my man but also towards society as a whole... You have the impression that everyone you meet knows about your situation...

So I called an addictologist in Nemours, and went back on medication.

We then went to stay with Clement's mom for a few days in May 2017. We had come back as well because she had to have surgery and we had to accompany her to the hospital. At her house we always drank more or less regularly. There were beers, homemade cider and then when it was not going well I would take the camper, with or without Clement, to find alcohol. He was really not happy with me, we often argued, but as I drank, I did not remember anything the next day.

You have to understand that alcohol was my oxygen... The first sip might be hard to take, it heats up, it burns, but I suddenly breathed and then I drank it like whey...

CHAPTER 23
LICENSE SUSPENSION AND WANDERING

On Friday, May 12, 2017, while I had left, already drunk, with the camper to buy vodka at the supermarket twenty minutes from the village, I received a call from the ASE informing me that Thimeo had run away from his foster family. I was told not to worry because he had phoned my father at the Dourdan train station to come and get him.

All I wanted to do was drown in alcohol. Thimeo had my father, but not his mother. Of course not: an alcoholic mother who lives in a camper van, you don't ask her for help.

In shock, I emptied the bottle of vodka I had... I wanted to forget everything... It was a disaster. I was answering the ESA under the influence of alcohol, to hear such serious news... which proved that my son knew he couldn't count on me.

I had only one objective, fed by a very strong determination: to go and get bottles of vodka to ease my pain, not to feel sorry for myself, nor for my son, just to forget.

When I entered the supermarket, I took my two bottles and I must not have been walking very straight. I certainly had the keys of the camper in my hands, so the cashier gave the alarm when she saw me leaving the store. A few minutes later I realized that I was being followed by the police on a small road, I stopped nicely, I knew that they were there for me... that I was "done".

Their breathalyzer didn't work and as I hadn't committed any offence in twelve years of driving, they drove me back to the village and asked me to stay there and not to move. They took my license and asked me to come and get it the next day at the police station.

But as soon as they left, as I needed alcohol and I couldn't remember where I had hidden the bottles, I took the camper van back to go to another store. Obviously they were waiting for me at the turn... I had to park the vehicle at the side of the road and go to the drunk tank... License retention and all the disasters that follow, DNA, fingerprints, tattoo photos, face and profile photos and the famous breathalyzer in which I had trouble blowing... That's it, I was on file. Then interrogation and drunk tank until the next day. The drunk tank is a raised concrete bed, a smelly hole for the toilet, it's disgusting and that's all... The big closed door with a giant lock, it's disproportionate and it's scary... The only thing you can do to make the time go by faster is to lie down on the blanket and sleep...

Meanwhile, the police called Clement and my father, who was not happy at all, to come and get me the next day.

Clément didn't have a license, so I had to deal with my father...

What was the future going to be like? The motorhome was our home... Even on wheels, it was our home.

But still no *click*. Alcoholism makes you put things into perspective, so I thought this was my first arrest. You manage to put everything into perspective, even if you know that you are acting in bad faith...

My father arrived furious, Clement was overwhelmed. I went out after getting something to smoke and I let my father take it out on the cops... not on me. I didn't want to hear it, I had just spent a night in the gnouf, I wanted to breathe.

This withdrawal of license came at a very bad time because we had to accompany Clément's mother to the hospital a few days later for her operation and it was no longer possible. Clément was and still is angry with me. Once again my alcoholism did not allow us to do what we had talked about. And this was important. I was ashamed towards his mother. It is quite impossible to rely on someone with this alcoholic disease. Everyone blames her and we feel guilty too, but we lose the trust of our loved ones, we have no credibility and that's normal. We live hour after hour, day after day. We don't know how the next day will go, how we will be able to drink, and then thinking about the future makes us dizzy...

The alcohol had worked well, so it wasn't until my father arrived that I remembered my son had run away. My father was in a state and if he could have given me a beating, he would have done it, I am sure. He took us back to Clément's mother's house in the village, and then he left.

I decided to spend the night in the camper and I found the bottles that were hidden there... From the first sip I felt relieved of these emotions. I got drunk again until I fell asleep. Clément was not far away, we were making head but he left me alone and I, finally I felt admiring of Thimeo to have had the courage to flee the foster family and to go to my parents.

We stayed for a while with Clement's mother to help her with the daily routine, but she was starting to be afraid of me. She was disappointed and certainly worried about her son being with a girl like me. And then there was always a neighbor who came over for a drink at the house and I took advantage of it, I would have a little beer from time to time.

When her mother was almost cured, we had to leave, she did not want us to stay, she did not want me to stay. She was in the process of selling her house but we couldn't take care of anything... My friend had to leave things that were important to him behind. Leaving his sister to deal with the move. Again I have my share of responsibility... And these are things that cannot be changed...

As I didn't have the license anymore, we looked for a plan to park somewhere for a long time. We found the camping of Sens. It is Clément who took the risk to drive there. And we fell well: two steps from the supermarket! How many evenings I screwed up ? I didn't stop drinking.... It was white from morning to night, and when I could drink vodka I did it... We stayed there two months.

At that time I could drink two bottles of vodka a day... We lived next door to a nice bum whose friends from the ZUP came to visit him every day. I was almost at the bottom of the social ladder. We had water, electricity, but we were stuck, we couldn't drive... It was the downfall, the total social fall, but we still had a "house"... We were still at home, sheltered from the bad weather.

We had to make a round trip to see Thimeo at the ASE, by hitchhiking and Blablacar... It was constraining: tired, under alcohol or medication, walking, hitchhiking, carpooling and pretending everything was fine... It was morally wearing.

While we were in Sens, I did everything I could to get my license back: psycho test, blood tests, dematerialized photo... Even if I kept on drinking, my tests were good, but I had more trouble with the psycho test because my neurons were a bit fried.

I couldn't stand being at the campground, with the bums as neighbors, who I passed on my way to the store and they were panhandling... I was almost on their level. And I couldn't stand that idea. I explained the situation to my parents and they allowed us to go to the country house. It was a relief. Without a license, it was Clément who took the risk of driving to the Nièvre.

We moved there, we started to do gardening and structural work because there was work to be done, no one had done it for a long time. I was very active and invested in it, but we were surrounded by people who drank a lot, wine, Ricard and whisky... I drank as much as the others, even more... We always had alcohol at home. These "friends" would come in the evening, and the cubi would go through four of them, knowing that there was often "the little yellow one" before. And then I would get my vodka as often as possible.

Jacques, a compassionate neighbor in the village, took us shopping once or twice a week. From time to time I would go alone with him and buy some vodka which I would drink in the parking lot before throwing the bottle in a trash can. I would hide another one on me, but I would get burned by Clément. Nothing changed...

Anyway, the more I drank, the less I could hold my liquor... During this period we still drank good wine, because we had access to my father's cellar! We emptied it a little; when my father noticed it he was obviously not very happy.

On September 1st, 2017 we went to harvest again, it was my father who accompanied us in the Beaujolais. Unlike the first time, I could not keep up, it was too hard, the atmosphere was not there and we were very badly housed. So we left after two days, without any regret, but as far as I was concerned, a certain feeling of guilt... It was me who was not keeping up, and yet I was doing my best. I went to see the boss and told him that I was going to stop, that I wasn't keeping up with the pace, and he had the nerve to tell Clément that he could stay but that I was useless. Clément did not give up and we left together. We hitchhiked with our big bags to the country house.

Chapter 24
The Breakdown, the December 24, 2017 Nod and woofing

I continued to drink but wine mainly, as I needed to get my blood tests done in preparation for the medical check-up that was going to take place in Nanterre on Monday November 13, 2017. I was finally able to get my license back for a one year probationary period. We then took a hotel room in Paris, at F1 de la porte de Châtillon, because I had an appointment with Thimeo on November 15 at the ASE.

Still unstable in the eyes of everyone, the fact that we were in the country with my parents, that we didn't work on a daily basis, all this didn't give confidence to Thimeo, nor to the ladies of the ASE. I knew that my son was happy to be with his grandparents and that he had the permission of the judge to stay there.

We hitchhiked back to the Nièvre, but with the license in my pocket, it was a new lease on life... Finally! I swore to myself that even if I continued to drink, I would never again drive under the influence of alcohol. It's strange but I was more afraid of losing my license than I was of causing an accident. It's very selfish to think like that and irresponsible but it's the truth.

So we took the camper again... We went to Orange, Aix-en-Provence, Port-Saint-Louis and then we went to see a cousin of Clément near Bourges. We stayed there for a few days before coming back to Plessis-Robinson to come to Paris, this time for the hearing with the Juvenile Judge.

In December 2017, the ASE declared itself incompetent for Thimeo and there was the affirmation of the AEMO measure in my parents' home. As usual Julio was absent at the hearing.

We had not run the motorhome for two days and when we left, it was impossible to start it again... So I called the repairman who tried to start it with Start Pilot but without success. He dropped us off at a garage in Bagneux where the mechanic studied the problem and thought he could fix it but by ordering a special part, all this in the middle of the holiday season. As soon as we got our license back, we couldn't really enjoy it. Fortunately we were well parked, not too far from the cemetery to get water nor too far from the stores. At first we thought it was a matter of a few days but in reality we stayed there for two months.

Since it was the holiday season I was really flooded with sadness. I drank to compensate for the tears that were flowing in my heart. Knowing that my son was so close and not being able to see him since he was now in a foster home with my parents was heartbreaking. I felt more and more abandoned. I couldn't even go to my parents' house anymore because Thimeo was there.

They all went to the mountains where they were lent an apartment and we, for Christmas 2017, were stuck in Bagneux. Clement and I bought wine, oysters and then as I needed more, I went to get some vodka against my friend's advice, but it was Christmas. Ah... the Christmas holidays when you are separated from your family, from your son... It could not go well, I was at my worst inside. I messed up everything, I let myself go, I went crazy because I was so drunk that I called the police for assault and battery on the part of Clément when it was me who had sought him out; in the end he spent the night in prison... I was in a bad way... I couldn't be well during this holiday season. The police called me the next day to see if I wanted to press charges. I was shocked to have put him through this, especially on a New Year's Eve, but I was morally exhausted: after the driving ban, the truck that dropped us, the family celebrations I was deprived of... Once again, Clément was the receptacle of all my frustrations, sorrows and alcoholic angers...

In the situation we were in, I finally thought about woofing. The only solution was to go to someone who had a place where we could stay in exchange of some services... So we ended up woofing in Alençon with a guy, Titoff, who, driving trucks, knew enough to repair ours... and with whom alcohol was flowing freely.

It was the shock, there was not only the nature, the animals and the repair of the truck, every evening it was "pastis party" and the bottle passed there without any problem... With the other woofers, it was: strong beers the day, pastis and sangria the evening. We were with real alcoholics.

Clement was trying hard not to drink, but when I caught him, I was overcome by this need, it wasn't jealousy but simply the lack of the product in my brain and body... I couldn't handle it. It put me in a bad mood, and it was obviously Clément who suffered from it.

Our house on wheels, our "trailer" as my brother once said, needed to be repaired and this was the only place where we could do it. As it was going to last for a long time, I asked to be followed at the hospital in Alençon by a psychiatrist specialized in addictology and by a psychologist. I managed to stay clean for a month despite the context... It didn't last though, there was too much alcohol around me.

I started drinking again, and drinking so much that one night when I wanted to have alcohol again, I don't know what came to mind, but I took the bottle of bleach and put it in my mouth.

And then, the black hole. I know that my friend called the fire department and that I was tied up in a hospital I didn't know...

Chapter 25
The "Vodkarian" Escape from the Hospital Center of Mayenne

So I woke up in the hospital without knowing where I was... Strapped down like never before. Having forgotten everything about the previous evening.

After a while the doctor comes back with a nurse. She told me that no, I would not be discharged for four or five hours at the end of the day, even though the day had not yet begun. It was going to be a long, long time, and it seemed unthinkable. I had to stay for observation, but I found that unnecessary. Staying in this hallway, with no one around for twelve hours? What good was that going to do? I would be better off at home sleeping and resting. The only good news was that the doctor allowed the nurse to untie me completely. She took out her famous magic magnet and removed the ties that had made me an insane person in a cuckoo's nest... What a relief! I felt alive again... A light and delicious wind of freedom made all my senses wriggle... Freedom starts here, not to be tied to anything or anyone, unless you want to be!

After a while I get up and walk a little beside my stretcher to stretch my legs, wrists and back... To regain a sense of space around me by detaching myself from this pillory... Finally, out of curiosity and with a clearer and clearer mind, I go to the end of the corridor, slowly, without making any noise, in my socks, my senses alert.

I watch all the deserted corridors, like a stalked animal because I know that if I am untied it is not to visit, to come and go where I want and to get away... I am risking a lot, and I absolutely do not want to be tied up again. I look in the rooms where the complaints came from but I see nothing, it is too dark. All my senses are awake, I can smell the patients, the nurses' coffee, the noises....

After the corner of the corridor, the glass is transparent. I finally find the nurses' room and I look carefully at their faces. I look for the one who looks the most sympathetic but without being too young, otherwise it could be a student who often has to go to her superior. I observe everything... The doctor being still there, I make myself discreet, I return towards my stretcher and decide to wait that she leaves. I lie down on the only "bed of the corridor" and I wait.

Deep down, I really want to smoke and I can't imagine staying there all day! I don't have the urge to smoke but I don't like being told what to do!

It's still dark, I still don't know what time it is because I didn't ask but I think it must be around four or five in the morning.

Lying down, I look at the corner of the corridor, at the ceiling and above all I take advantage of the possibility to move each of my limbs, I bend my legs, turn my wrists, and I try to comb my hair, which is sticky with alcohol, in order to look like something again. I am aware that I have to look better, I pinch my cheeks to get some color... Alcohol makes you look pale.

I'm impatient, I want to smoke, and I'm pissed at the doctor. I want to smoke and I want to get out of here. I go back to the nurses' station, in my socks, without making a sound. The doctor is gone but the nurse is there and she doesn't look like a student. Sympathy-wise, I'll see, I decide to take a chance and tap on the office window.

The nurse goes out. I tell her I want to smoke... She doesn't mind since she sees me standing, stable... She goes back into her office, gives me my shoes, my coat ("because it's cold outside") and asks me to rummage through my bag, which she keeps, so that I can take a cigarette and a light. She tells me how to get to the smoking area. I go calmly, I have the authorization, I take advantage of it... I already put my coat on as a reassuring protection against this place. I take several corridors and I arrive in a big hall. Not a sound around me, on the left a transparent door that leads to a courtyard, a place between four walls. I sit down on a bench and it's true that it's cold - thanks for the coat ma'am! - I smoke and observe what surrounds me... I am still locked up, but I smoke and breathe, I feel the fresh wind on my face. What a relief, what softness!

When the cigarette is finished, I look for a few butts that can still be smoked to make the moment last. By dint of being in hospitals I learned to rummage in public ashtrays to smoke other people's butts... When you have no choice, you're happy to find some!

As I walk into the lobby, I notice a glass door that looks like the exit to the hospital. But... I... I can't do that, I am a prisoner of the doctor's authority. By habit, one obeys the doctor in a white coat... It's the authority... and above all I don't have my bag... So it's not the right time: no rushing and no false steps.

I go back to the nurses' station and give back my shoes, my coat and the lighter... I find my stretcher of death... I have just come back and already the time seems long. After a very long time, I go back to the nurse to ask where the toilets are... And while going there, I take my small air, I ask her to go to smoke again by saying to her that as I saw beside the smoking room of what to take a coffee I would like to have my bag in which are some coins.

What is clear at this precise moment, it is that she is in confidence and moreover she must be occupied by something else. She gives me her consent, gives me back my shoes, my coat and my bag! I tell her I'm going to smoke a couple, have a coffee, don't worry, I'll be right back... I put my shoes, coat and bag back on my shoulder... I go back to the corridor, I take the coffee, I smoke a cigarette in the smoking room... And there, I know that I have everything with me, that freedom is on the other side of the glass. It's irresistible, the great hall is empty, I come out of the smoking room, and I check that there is nobody there. I go towards the transparent door, towards the exit, I don't look behind me. As naturally as possible I approach the electric door, it opens, I pass... That's it, I'm out of the building. It's cold but I'm hot, I'm all excited.

Outside, I see a straight road in the distance, a few cars parked on the sides of the hospital, and in front of me small paths that look like they are used by pedestrians to get to the road. I feel the cool wind on my face. I move, I walk, now I am free... Free to go straight... Towards life, the city. The world that continues to turn.

I think I hear a nurse calling me back but I don't turn around; I continue, I trace my road without accelerating... That's it I see the traffic circle: on the right a supermarket (when I see it I can't help it, the word "vodka" resounds in me) but it is closed of course. I would certainly have gone there because in my state nothing stops me. In front of me, a suburban area and a highway; on the right it is the direction of the city center and on the left the exit of the city... It is still early, maybe half past seven. I decide to go to the left because I don't recognize Alençon at all... I will hitchhike, I have to leave this city...

So I walk quickly on the sidewalk and there it is magic, invisible from far but getting closer it is indeed that: a coffee! And it's open! 500 meters from the hospital! Unbelievable! I push the door, I order a coffee and ask the lady where I am... I am in Mayenne at one hour by car from where we repair our motor home...

In spite of my head of this day of found freedom, with my not very sure gestures, the waitress gives me some telephone numbers of cabs, which I call frantically. I find one that is available to pick me up at 9 o'clock. I ask for the address of the café where I am, and I sit down in a corner where I cannot be seen from the outside, I drink my coffee... I have sensations that frighten me a little, I tremble slightly, I am on the alert... I do not feel stable at all because I am in the forbidden and the infraction. The truth is that I am a bit scared and above all I am in a state of withdrawal...

Chapter 25 The "Vodkarian" Escape from the Hospital Center of Mayenne

I'm not going to ask the waitress for a vodka, the hospital is next door and she must have their phone number, I'm in a risk zone... I must not be too badly hurt so that she doesn't give the alarm...

And there the alcohol drawer opens again in my head. Having seen this store, it starts again, I don't think anymore: the stress of having run away, the anxiety of leaving and the anxiety of coming home... No medicine... I feel that I am weak. I need a booster, I need alcohol, I need vodka.

Why vodka? Because it's the most effective alcohol, the least smelly and I'm used to it, I know its effects and at what doses.

So with an innocent look I ask the lady at the café:

- What time does the supermarket open?

- Half past eight...

I look at the clock on the wall. It opens in less than ten minutes but I know that I would take risks because it is necessary to cross the traffic circle of the entrance of the hospital to go there... OK, anyway, my animal instinct and this vision of alcohol at hand are the strongest and the solution to my anxieties... I signal to the lady of the coffee shop that I am going to the supermarket and that I come back quickly, if the cab arrives, let it wait for me.

I cover myself and I go out, it is still dark at this hour and it rains... I go back to the hospital. On the crosswalk, I lower my head, I pass, I continue along the road and I arrive at the supermarket still fenced... I have just the time to smoke a cigarette before it opens. I'm the first customer and I'm in a hurry because I'm afraid to run into hospital staff, you never know. I go to the full yoghurt aisle, then I take a small bottle of water and I finally go to the aisle I've been waiting for since the beginning - I couldn't go there first, it was too visible - the one of the strong alcohols and there, I take it: a big bottle of vodka... Not small nor medium, a big one! I know that it goes fast with me and I want to have some left for my return. It reassures me, it's my crutch.

Of course, I tell myself that it's not right, that the bottle is a poison, but I also know that I will feel better anyway. It's like curing evil with evil. If only I could do without it, but I can't... The hold and the need are as much psychological as physical.

I am waiting for the cashier, here he comes. He is long. I know it's still a bit early but I'm in a hurry. In a hurry to get back to the café and in a hurry to drink my magic potion. I pay, it rains, I put the bottle of vodka in my bag. And my hood.

I go back the way I came, it's raining more and more, I lower my head and I'm about to cross when, from the corner of my eye, I see a car to which I have to give way at the traffic circle. And there, I recognize it, it is the doctor, incredible! It is still dark, and as she has never seen my silhouette with my coat and my hood, she does not recognize me. She starts again and leaves. She didn't look at me, I was a shadow on the sidewalk in the wet night.

I continue towards the bistro. I hurry, alert like a hunted animal and guilty of buying this poison I need so much to calm down. I enter the bar, I recommend a coffee, I put my water bottle on the table and my big yoghurt and I run to the toilet to drink my vodka... I drink, I swallow the alcohol (I don't mind it) and I count to ten, I know that at the neck it's already a good quantity, I'm used to it... I flush the toilet to be credible...

Chapter 25 The "Vodkarian" Escape from the Hospital Center of Mayenne

And I am already feeling the effects. It is immediate! That's it, I'm lighter. I "breathe" again, I have had my fill. I finally feel calm, almost peaceful and serene, ready to wait for the cab. I force myself to eat my yogurt, I hope that it will make me feel good to have something else in my stomach. I observe a couple and two children sitting two tables away from me... They are regulars of the house, they know the owner. The children look at me. They come to have breakfast and they observe me. They are almost insistent but once again I don't care what they think, the main thing is in my bag. It's been a long time that I don't care about the others' look when I buy alcohol... Grocery store, supermarket, restaurant. Nothing to do; I assume! But now, they are not supposed to know that I ran away from the hospital, I'm just a stranger passing by, a little bit weird, that's all.

However, the risk is permanent. They must have the number of the hospital at the café... I must not be the first nor the last to take the powder. This proves that I didn't look too bad.

A few more minutes before the cab arrives, I go back to the bathroom, take my bottle and count to ten... I straighten the bottle and I see that I have already downed it, but it's not a big deal as long as there is still some left...

The cab finally arrives, I get in it, towards the camper and my friend... I am drunk but saved from the clutches of the hospital that wanted to keep me... I feel protected in the cab even if I have the fear in my stomach to find what my life has become and that I don't like. Because I didn't belong anymore, and I didn't belong anywhere... I didn't like what I was going to find, the state of the words and things I had to leave behind in my alcoholic madness. I knew I would have some explaining to do, and some apologizing to do...

In the meantime and thinking about it, it's still crazy: I run away from the hospital, I find a supermarket, I find an open bar and I have the nerve to go and get some vodka by crossing the hospital traffic circle three times! I was scared to death but I did it. Anyway, as soon as I saw the store, I couldn't help myself. When you're an alcoholic, the whole world can go to hell, the important thing is the bottle... And on top of that, you think you're strong and clever.

When we arrived, the people where we had put the camper wanted us to leave because of my fault. However, we couldn't leave our house there, broken down at Titoff's who promised to fix it. He ended up replacing our engine and in the meantime I took care of the eggs, the chickens and the kids.

It was hard to take care of the children, there was a four year old and a seven year old... When this one was from behind, I felt like I was seeing my son and it brought tears to my eyes... Where was he? What was he doing? I wanted to go back to the time when we were happy, but it was impossible. I saw the happiness of others and it brought me back to my maternal distress, making me want to drink to bury my feelings and to support my new daily life.

When you are in this situation of coming back ashamed after having made a mess, it is hard to ask for forgiveness, maybe because you know deep down that you will do it again when the opportunity will come. So apologizing when the damage is done and you know, that everyone suspects, that there will be a next time, is useless... But you do it anyway, with an assumed hypocrisy.

Chapter 25 The "Vodkarian" Escape from the Hospital Center of Mayenne

A question arises: and the *click*, where is it? How does it come? Is it someone who gives it to you, do you have to find it by yourself? How far do you have to go to find it? The loss of values, the loss of trust of your loved ones, rejection, abandonment, anger, sadness, accidents, the street, decay, death are easier to find than this fucking *click*!!!

It's still a world away because before I was registered in the calendar of the psychiatrist of Alençon, we had gone there with Clément, without an appointment, saying "it's urgent, I need you! Right away, I'm ready, I need to treat myself! And we were told that we would have an appointment as soon as possible, in two or three weeks... One can die, kill, hurt, hurt oneself a hundred times in three weeks when one drinks to the point of being insane! I really wanted to get out of it and I felt rejected by the system... As if my case wasn't urgent. But it was. Distress should be taken seriously and treated immediately. It's a form of suicide to drink so much... And then you hear yourself say "you'll have an appointment in three weeks"? But that may be too late, buddy! I need help now, as long as I am ready and still alive... Besides, the addictology building in Alençon is located right next to the crematorium... A whole program...

So we left... Clément was angry... and I was confused, angry too and sad. So sad. I was a lost person, I felt at the end of my life. And I missed my son's love so much... But anyway, he wouldn't have liked to see me like that.

And there it was, after a while, this one more relapse. I was told what I had done, that I was so drunk that I took the bottle of bleach and drank it... I don't know if I actually drank it because I didn't get my stomach pumped or have any physical consequences...

It was always Clément who was there to tell me what had happened and to try to make me face the reality of my problem. It's true that even though he had to endure a lot for two years, he was always there for me, even if he didn't mince his words. It is clear that he does not realize how strong my addiction is and how guilty and ashamed I feel... Everyone around me is helpless in front of this problem that is alcoholism... And when I drink, I do not remember anything. Absolutely nothing, it's a black hole, a complete blackout.

Chapter 26
HP or weaning?...
Withdrawal ma'am! Mamers!

As soon as the truck started working again we fled the woofing, because after the bleach episode, the atmosphere was not the same anymore. After a two days break next to a lake we settled in Alençon on a parking lot, so that I would not be far from the hospital where I was followed by the addictologist.

But I kept going and that's all I could think about... drinking! It was sabotage, self-destruction; I even kicked out Clement who left "permanently". I was texting and texting him insults, drunk and wasted. The truck was malfunctioning, but I continued to drink and find enough energy to go buy alcohol. I found myself alone, with no water or electricity, and therefore no phone... I destroyed everything in the truck, broke a bottle of vodka on the pine table, varnished by us. As I couldn't get into the nasturtium anymore, I started to sleep on the floor. The floor was sticking because of the vodka, but at this point I didn't care.

I believe that it was my mother who, from Paris, phoned the fire department... They came and took me to the hospital in Alençon. There they let me rest and then the doctor warned me: it was either a two-week withdrawal in Mamers (a center twenty kilometers from Alençon) or the psychiatric hospital. So on my stretcher I answered: "Withdrawal, ma'am!

So on April 16, 2018 here I am leaving the hospital in Alençon in a wheelchair, in an open gown on my back. I had only my bag and the clothes I was wearing in a hospital bag... Arrived in Mamers a nice guy lent me underwear, jogging, T-shirt, socks and a lady, a towel.... I rushed to take a good shower and to get dressed normally. I was ashamed, my legs were covered with bruises.

In this conventional nursing home, the alcoholics shared a hallway with the terminally ill. Since I was not scheduled, they found me a place in the room of one of them, who did not speak and had respiratory problems... This meant being subjected to the noise of the machine and believe me, it makes a lot of noise, especially when you are in withdrawal and any noise is unbearable... So there I was for a couple of weeks, away from everyone... I was able to charge my phone but I had no news from my friend, I didn't dare call him either. I was thinking that this time it's really over... I was sad but I accepted my fate...

As I didn't have many clothes, I bought some on the internet... Little by little I was getting back into my feminine shape, without any fuss given the place. I was tired, exhausted and being with the dying did not make me feel better. At night the nurses put me on a mattress on the floor in a meeting room to spare me the noise of the machine, not to mention the smells of the room... It made many people laugh that I had to sleep on the floor in a room at the end of the corridor.

As a patient, we were free to move around and I was the good student, I actively participated in activities, nutrition, cigarettes, various drinks and meetings with associations.... But these associations are only made up of relatively old people, whereas we patients are rather young... Once again, it was not adapted.

After a while I got a room, with a lady who talked a lot and always about alcohol. I was getting tired and wanted something else for myself, so I asked to change rooms and the lady decided to leave because she felt abandoned...

I called my parents. I was far from Paris but they came. They got into the camper and contacted a mechanic to come and pick it up. They were able to get me some clothes and clean it up a bit. They also brought me my car so that I could go back to the Nièvre region at the end of the weaning. I felt good in their company... I started to realize that I was tired of being an alcoholic... The day they left they told me about Thimeo who was with his uncle, they showed me his notebook from the fifth grade when we were on the bench in the sun. Then we ran into this lady who had chosen to leave the withdrawal because I had changed rooms... She was drunk. It was sad to see her like that and my parents took the opportunity to tell me, "You see where alcohol leads..." Yes, I already knew that.

One day I received a phone call and I knew that Clément was in the Nièvre region, staying with friends... I wondered what I was going to do with my life, thinking that it was really over with him, wondering where I was going to go. I didn't want to stay there, but thanks to the social worker in Mamers, I had applied for low-cost housing in Alençon, in the Hauts-de-Seine...

The two-week treatment was about to end, my luggage had been packed since the evening before, I was thinking about Clément, my parents and my son... and I knew that I was going to drive more than 300 kilometers on my own again. I was apprehensive about going back but I was happy, it's true that I was getting better. I left Mamers, I filled up my tank, I went into a store to buy a USB key to charge my phone with the cigarette lighter and I couldn't help it, it was a reflex, I bought some vodka for my return.

I didn't touch it until I got within five kilometers of the house where Clément was. The weather was beautiful, it was spring, almost summer, the rape fields were all yellow. The area is hilly, it was really beautiful.

Five kilometers before arriving, I started to drink again. And I immediately felt a little more confident to meet Clément. He believed, hoped that I had changed, that I had *clicked* this time... But no. He thought I was behaving strangely and he was right. But I did not say anything.

Deep inside I was very anxious, not because I had alcohol with me, on the contrary it reassured me, but at the idea of having to recover the truck in Alençon, not completely repaired nor completely broken down... And then what to do afterwards, to go back on the road ? To go where and do what? The questions kept coming back... and I was far from my son even if he didn't want to see me. I was still lost.

So we moved back to the country, and Clément phoned one of his cousins so that he and his wife would take us to Alençon with my car and we would come back with the truck.

It is Clément who drove once more and fortunately for us all went well... We made the round trip in one day.

Chapter 27
The logical continuation:
the psychiatric hospital

There, everything accelerated...

I was very bad. When I drank, I would scream in the garden. The neighbors, even from a distance, could hear me, they were worried. I ended up in the hospital in Clamecy where they know me well: I had to go there in a state of alcoholism at least four or five times, with or without the firemen. After a little rest, the hospital let me go back by cab.

It was a lady, the cab. I sat in front and knowing the road, I knew we were going to pass a supermarket. I told her that I was thirsty, that I needed some sugar, some cola. I asked her if she wanted anything and we stopped at the store. The first aisle I went to was the liquor aisle, then the Coke aisle... I hid the bottle of vodka in my bag and went home.

Of course we had discussions with Clément, but as soon as his back was turned, I took a few sips. At the end of the day, he realized that something was wrong. So I told him the truth... and it happened again, I went back to the hospital:

same cab, same stop at the store... But this time my friend searched my stuff: caught red-handed.

Since I was in withdrawal from alcohol, I called to go to a treatment center in Decize, in the region, and I was accepted the very next day.

I wanted to drink and the nurse on the phone agreed to get me some vodka, as I was going back to the center the next day... The same day I didn't want to go anymore, I wanted to get out of the moving car, my friend held me back. I finally stayed there only one day. It was one more withdrawal... I was free to leave since I had come of my own free will.

I am attached to the Nièvre, it is a part of my childhood and I had found there a certain balance, certainly alcoholic but I was trying to drink less and to enjoy nature. I worked hard in the garden with Clément, even if the booze was always there: a bottle of wine at lunchtime and/or a few beers and a bottle of wine in the evening. When you're an alcoholic like me, you're frustrated that you can't drink more, it was a feeling that never left me, and the 13% of alcohol wasn't enough for me, it didn't fool me at all.

I continued to drink... On May 28, 2018, still under the influence of alcohol, I started screaming, I was screaming suicide... I was rolling on the ground in the backyard, in a completely unconscious state, I was no longer myself. The alcohol had made me crazy and suicidal, I was saying, "I want to die, I want to die".

The neighbors and Clément, more than worried, called the firemen, the deputy mayor even came and I went once again to the hospital in Clamecy. They left me alone, I could go and smoke cigarettes and I asked when I could go out... I didn't have any answer but I was doing pretty well after this binge... Then two ladies from the social services came and told me that they were sending me to a specialized unit in La Charité-sur-Loire. At the time I didn't quite understand what that meant... I was waiting nicely, I was infused but I kept going to smoke with my hospital gown on. A nurse came and took all my stuff. That was a bad sign, I could only keep my personal bag but no shoes: the hospital gown and sheet on me, that's all. I was put on a stretcher in an ambulance for what seemed like a very long ride.

So I entered a psychiatric hospital with a decision of admission in psychiatric care in case of imminent danger in the absence of a third party on May 29, 2018 in La Charité sur Loire.

We arrive in front of a sordid building, the nurses of the ambulance press on a bell and on the other side of the door in ice, a nurse comes, with a huge bunch of keys, to open a first door, then a second one with another key so that we can enter. This was no longer a hospital like the others, I was in a psychiatric hospital, I saw it immediately by looking at the other patients. I was very afraid.

They searched my things, took out all the cables, phone charger, music headphones, cigarettes, lighters, my medication and my pill, and then they explained to me that because I had been hospitalized too many times in Clamecy and because I was talking about suicide, I had been placed here at the request of a third party. I immediately asked for a copy

Chapter 27 The logical continuation: the psychiatric hospital of the document because it was out of the question that I stay there. I'm an alcoholic: I'm not schizophrenic or crazy or bipolar. I'm just full of sadness but I love life too much to end it on my own, even if I drink myself to death. It was desperation, a real and deep cry of despair.

The building was dilapidated, there was a big glass roof at the end of a huge and long corridor, which allowed us to sit and look outside. We could take smoke breaks every hour until 10pm but we had to stand in line to be given cigarettes and fire. I was shocked because to go smoke you needed big keys to open the door. The young people were either very excited or very quiet and deeply depressed. Some were haggard; others, with their mouths hanging open, were barely walking. You could see the effect of some of the treatments, which must have been very heavy, I didn't want to become like that, so I was very suspicious of what I was given.

The upstairs rooms were left open, of course there were robberies, intrusions... It's hard to rest when you're only allowed to get fresh air and smoke a cigarette once an hour and everything is closed. The windows of the rooms did not open... I was obviously watched closely when I went to smoke, when I wandered in the corridors and through the window that gave onto my room. They also had to watch who I was talking to, my behavior, my response.

I saw the psychiatrist, a Russian woman, who told me "OK, you'll stay there for three days and if a member of your family comes to get you, you can leave". So I ran to phone my mother to ask her to come and free me from this place which was a pure and hard confinement, medicalized and with more or less dangerous people... She told me that they would come in three days. I insisted because it was not at all adapted to me, who is alcoholic but not crazy. They are not the same pathologies.

How long the time seemed to me! Contrary to a cure, there is no activity... and there it was not me who was looking for the butts in the ashtrays, it was the old ones. As in the other centers, there were patients who came back regularly for more or less long periods, others who didn't know when they were going to leave and who didn't care... Oh dear, I didn't want that for myself!

One of the long-time patients, who was a bit gruff, was there because he had attempted suicide after the death of his wife. When he went to see the psychiatrist, she would ask him if he realized what he had done and he would always say yes, and that if he did it again, he would do it again. This was not what the psychiatrist wanted to hear, he was advised to say something else, to say that he was sorry, but no, nothing to do, he would not give up. He was going to be there for a long time and he didn't mind.

Even in this HP, cigarette and lighter trafficking was common. Elders smoked in their rooms despite bans and searches. But they didn't care about breaking the law. They didn't plan to go out.

The day came when I had to leave, three days after my arrival, an eternity.

I say hello to my mother, my father doesn't even look at me... They go straight to the psychiatrist's office. They talk but I don't hear anything. I see my father get up, scream, and

Chapter 27 The logical continuation: the psychiatric hospital be kicked out by the nurses, after the two passes of the keys. I am shocked, I don't understand what happened.

I was invited to sit in the office with my mother, we held hands and the psychiatrist explained to me that my father was very angry that I was being let out, that I was sick and that if I went out I would drink again, so I explained that this was not my place as an alcoholic. The psychiatrist agreed and suggested that I stay the week. She suspends the placement at the request of a third party today, June 1st, 2018, on the condition that I actually stay for a week... Since I have no choice, I agree. She added that she couldn't do otherwise because my father, who smelled of pinard from twenty meters away, had threatened her and that he wasn't behaving normally. That it was because of this that I had to stay in this HP longer, that she didn't like the threats.

We leave the office, Mom stays with me for a while, but I want to spare her, the place is sad and gloomy, the patients are scary, the confinement is scary... The separation is painful, but it is better this way, for her and for me. She brought me several little things, including a book about the joy of living: *Vivre content* by Jean-Louis Servan-Schreiber.

In *Living content* the author talks about himself, to, obviously, talk about us. About our inability to take advantage of what is offered to us, about these projections into the future and these regrets of the past that prevent us from savoring the present moment. He does not pretend to give solutions, but proposes to "rely on the positive aspects of what happens to us at any time". He dwells on the family, "the breeding ground of our neuroses". All this to understand that we cannot change the world and its reality, but that the work towards "contentment" is to accept and manage it in order to live it as little violently as possible... To bring about the luck we expect from others. We find ourselves smiling, hoping, making good resolutions.

Her book helped me a lot to understand how lucky I was to be alive and healthy... I was counting every minute that passed. And the book allowed me to pass the time by finding some hope in this very brutal and violent world, it opened my eyes to my life that I could still change. It made me realize that it is never too late.

During the week I spent in the hospital, I realized that there were also old people who didn't belong there, who should be in a nursing home. The poor things were bent over their plates and hardly moved at all. The staff didn't take care of them, they were patients who helped them to eat and not to choke on the food.

Then one night, there was a lot of noise. When it's like that, it's better not to go out... It was someone who had just committed suicide...

Yes, death was everywhere here... Medicated, deprived of freedom, no more contact with the elements and life, locked up, the sound of keys and doors that open quickly and close even faster, watched over by little bosses who have all the power over you. The best thing is not to go in. It's worse than prison because once you're in, you don't know if you'll ever get out. There is no release date, the psychiatrists have all the power and can easily change their mind about your situation.

When I was in the hallways, I looked at the hospital rules and under the beneficial influence of my book, I realized that having this "psychiatric care termination decision" document dated June 1st, 2018, I was within my rights to ask to leave early, to ask the psychiatrist to let me go despite the week I had to spend here.

I had two days left and I knew that every minute I spent in this place was time that was stolen from my life. That it was legitimate after these realizations that I wanted to leave and take my life in hand, to be free again, far from this place so distressing. So I waited for the doctor who had to guess why I was staying in front of his office but who did not want to see me. I waited for her until she came out and told her that I wanted to leave. That I had the right to do so. I told her my arguments very calmly as I had done previously with the hospital staff to test if my request was legitimate or not, and it was according to the opinions I had had, the law being on my side... The shrink didn't say anything, she was accompanied by the head of the department who spoke to me in a very virulent tone, telling me that I had given my word that I would be discharged two days later and that changing the discharge date was out of the question. He even asked me if I had had anything to drink, told me that I had to stay calm because if I didn't, they were going to give me a placement at the request of a third party for a month!

I was flabbergasted, I couldn't believe my ears: already I was accused of having drunk something (one wonders what and how!) while I had an irreproachable behavior and extreme politeness, but on top of that I was threatened with a one month placement for a legitimate request! I quickly walked away from this conversation that I had wanted to be constructive and I understood how much power these people had over you by twisting the truth and threatening you without scruples within their establishment.

They were overstepping their rights, even though the patient's right was well posted in the establishment's charter... I was at their mercy. I was very afraid for myself. I was going to have to be patient and stay in this dangerous place. I was constantly on my guard, both with regard to the staff, whom I no longer trusted, and with regard to the patients, who could be unpredictable and violent at any moment.

I had Clement on the phone from time to time but I was beyond ashamed. I was in HP. I had reached a stage and, even though I didn't belong... I was there. So I didn't want to tell him too much about what I was going through, what I was seeing.

I couldn't let myself go. Because even if you are not crazy, in a place like this you can quickly become so. So I went back to my mother's book.

It was Clement and our dear neighbor, Jacques, who came to pick me up on the day of departure, June 5, 2018. I was in shock, and remained shocked by the experience for many months to come. I still think about it, I will be marked for life.

Chapter 28
Change alcohol
and go to the Vennery!

When I got out of the hospital, on June 5, 2018 I went to see the only doctor left in the area... I had asked that Clement could come with me for a consultation but the doctor invoked medical confidentiality... After prescribing me a few medications, he spoke frankly to me: if I was having trouble staying totally clean, I should turn to other alcohol but especially not touch vodka again.

I left the consultation all happy: I had the authorization to drink! I started drinking Ricard and then Suze. And I abused it! Every day, I drank a bottle of Suze, in addition to the wine. And I would go back, without scruples, to buy other bottles the next day: it was allowed and recommended by my doctor! Clément would have smashed his face in if he could. How could a doctor give such advice?

One day, my mother told me that since they didn't have enough money to go to the seaside, they would spend their vacations in the country house. Thimeo would be there and since he still didn't want to see me, we took refuge in the house where I grew up in the suburbs of Paris, where I had also drunk so much, where Thimeo's room was empty next to mine... All those memories... It was going to be hard to hold on. I couldn't help but drink again and again.

We were also taking care of the garden, which did not prevent me from drinking again, and I had a crisis. The firemen came, the police too, but it ended well: no hospital or prison for anyone.

When my Thimeo flew to Corsica for summer camp and then spent a week with his godmother, we joined my parents in the country. I don't remember how many shenanigans I pulled, or how I did it, but I was constantly on the lookout for alcohol. I managed to buy and drink it and was successful even when "supervised", even after high school. My dad would hide bottles that I found, in addition to the ones I drank on my own. My parents were overwhelmed, and Clement remembers how much his back hurt because I constantly had to go to the bathroom and he had to carry me. I couldn't walk because I was so drunk.

One day the firemen came to the house three times... but I stayed and they let me sleep.

With Clément, coming back to Paris was out of the question. We needed something else. So we took back the camper and we went to the Morvan, to the lake of Settons, where we spent good moments, in the peace... We still drank, but moderately... I always had the frustration to not be able to drink more. I would create problems so I could go to the store by myself to buy flasks of whiskey and stuff. I kept wasting all the happy moments. I was too unhappy: my son was a few kilometers away and I couldn't see him... Finally we decided to go back the day before to have a chance to meet Thimeo and give him a hug, but when we got there my father told me that it showed on my face that I had been drinking the day before and didn't want to go any further.

I continued to drink and drink... Everything except vodka as the doctor had advised me, but always with a view to forgetting, to putting myself on a break... Seeing my state my father finally went to meet this doctor who admitted that he was not a specialist in addictology. He did give him the address of two centers. We went to the first one but it was also a psychiatric hospital with big gates and a surveillance camera. They wouldn't let anyone in. Even the doctor couldn't see his own patients in this hospital, and he didn't know it himself.

The second facility, La Vennerie, was a retirement home that had opened an addiction unit. I agreed to go there, especially since they offered me the day hospital and to go home in the evening... However, I realized in two or three days that it was not going to be suitable. There were activities but once again it was not adapted to my pathology... I did not see how making bookmarks or a "therapy through work" by repainting the shutters could help me in my disease... Moreover I wanted a real follow-up with a psychologist, but the one of the center could not receive me and directed me towards an association. The same goes for the social worker. Even the addictologist couldn't give me a prescription because I was an outpatient. She asked me to go and see my super general practitioner... who was not competent in addictology... The snake was biting its own tail.

Then there was an information meeting about an association, the Anpaa, with a very nice, direct lady. I listened well to her, I liked her approach of the alcoholic disease and I went to see her. I called the next day to make an appointment with her and an addictologist, who still follow me every week. So I stopped the Vennerie, I also stopped seeing the doctor, and I decided to finally take care of myself, to come back to life by approaching this association, the Anpaa, where I was able to meet a competent addictologist who shows understanding of the disease, sympathetic to my story. I continue to see this lady who had promoted the association in La Vennerie. Little by little, by talking to both of them every week, I am regaining my self-confidence. I feel really encouraged in my definitive approach to alcohol.

But in fact this famous *click* I never had, or at least, it did not come to me as I thought.

Chapter 29
Abstinence: The Vision of a Whirlwind

Never since drinking came into my life had I been able to conceive of not drinking any alcohol in my entire life. It just seemed impossible.

The day before the miracle happened, I drank myself into a stupor, an argument broke out between Clement and me and I sold him the camper. I felt a great sense of release. It was as if I was beginning to turn a page on all the suffering - the ones I had experienced and the ones I had made him experience - since I refused this life choice.

That was November 18, 2018. Since then, I haven't touched a single drop of alcohol, nor have I ever wanted to.

The next morning, with my stomach churning and my head spinning, I went out into the garden and had a fainting sensation standing in front of the house, in the sun... A whirlwind in which I felt the alcohol burning my throat, damaging my body and head, my nervous system. I could smell the ambulances, the smells of the hospitals and their noises. I felt the straps that prevented me from moving... And

I saw alcohol, vodka, as the representative of hell, of sickness and imminent death with the feeling of lack so hateful and perilous. The vision of police, firemen, stretchers, straps and urinary catheters, confinement, time passing that I will never get back. All the disasters I escaped, in the car, in the camper, during the fights with Clément. The alcoholic madness, the fights, and my son that I didn't have anymore. My son, who was not doing well, who was no longer in school for his fourth year, the lack of staff, of educators to help him and my parents who were alone, not knowing what to do for my child...

This whirlwind of images, of feelings; these disillusions, this painful past, these sufferings, it was the famous *trigger*.

I was approaching my fortieth birthday, I didn't want to live through the hell of alcohol anymore, neither for myself nor for my loved ones. I went very far in alcoholism, I lost a lot: my son, my integrity, the trust that could be given to me. I caused a lot of pain and unhappiness to my family. My body, my head, didn't want it anymore... The alcohol box closed forever. This whirlwind gave me the courage and hope to become a pillar in my son's life again, to be there for him again. It's a realization that is with me 24 hours a day.

Clément's love is inseparable from this awareness and his support has been unfailing for two and a half years. Without him I would have died a long time ago... I think of all that he had to suffer for me, my Man, all those moments of solitude that my family, my son had to live. My son that I lost, who will never forgive me for all these pains and for having spoiled his life.

But I found again the pleasure to feel the wind in my hair, on my face, to hear the birds, to feel free. The happiness of being able to get up in the morning and remember what I did the day before. The desire and the possibility to rebuild myself, because with alcohol I had lost my self-confidence, the ability to manage my emotions... Gone is the courage that alcohol brings you, this illusion that the product gives you to be able to bear its infinite sadness. I am happy and the fear is no longer the same...

I would like to share with you one of my first victories. Not long ago I had a fight with my boyfriend. So I went shopping by myself, angry and sad, but with the wonderful satisfaction of not feeling the need for alcohol. I knew I was going to have just what we needed and nothing more. It had been five years since I had gone shopping alone without buying alcohol. It has happened again, and each time I get an unimaginable inner smile. The chapter is not closed but my total abstinence date is November 18, 2018 and I am alive and well, finding myself day by day.

I realized that the reason I drank so much was because I was not respected as a wife and mother by Julio and because of what happened to Thimeo at such a young age, the difficulty of being recognized as a victim... By knowing myself better, I managed to get out of alcohol. Before, I couldn't admit and accept the past.

I haven't heard from Julio in four years. He owes me 20,000 euros in unpaid alimony, and I know that I will never get it. The way society works is a disgrace for alimony payments because the CAF only allows for two years of retroactivity... But Julio will explain this to his son later... I don't want to let hatred and resentment take over. If someone asks me the question: "Did you choose alcohol over your son? I will answer, "No, that's not how it goes. One drowns one's sorrow when it is too great, and the road of psychological suffering was long before I plunged into this drug which is everywhere and easy to access: "hard drug", killer over the counter! After that it's the alcohol that drowns you... and nothing else exists. There is no choice at that point. There is only alcohol."

On December 12, 2018, the judgment was issued to renew Thimeo's AEMO placement. My son was without educators throughout the year. We had four or five in a year, but they were all interns. Their presence went from three weeks to three months, whereas we were promised a long term accompaniment each time. As at the ASE, the whole family met each one of them, putting all our hopes in them each time, telling our life story again and again, each time from the beginning because they changed all the time and did not seem to take the time to read Thimeo's file. The last one stayed until the hearing, so he had an educator that day, but she left shortly after, leaving us again in an institutional abuse, in the complete emptiness of an institution that does not have the means of its ambitions. This disturbs us but at the same time we are all, and first of all Thimeo, tired of these appointments, of going back to the past with strangers when we would like to resume a normal life without all these obligations and justifications to bring...

When Thimeo arrived at the court in front of the judge, I was able to express myself and open my heart to him. When he came out he hugged me tightly and asked me to come home for lunch. He then came to the country for a few days. We spent time together in a way we hadn't for so long. He saw that I didn't drink anymore and thanked Clément for taking good care of me... But he also understood that I wouldn't come back to live in Paris. He is still in doubt about the personal and professional path I will take, feeling that we are still unstable since with Clément we occupy my parents' country house. Nothing really secure for him. But we lived three days of reunion, and it was great.

There was also Christmas, where Thimeo wished we were there with the whole family. I refused to bring the bottles of wine that my father had asked me to buy and Thimeo could see that despite the people drinking around me, I was doing very well. I had made arrangements: there was no way I was going to be alone in the kitchen with almost empty glasses so I wouldn't set that box in my brain again. Anyway, I had prepared myself for it and I had in a way deprogrammed my gestures and my brain. Finally a moment with my family, all together. How heartwarming!

Then there was his birthday: Thimeo turned fourteen on January 11, 2019. We spent his birthday together then went to a Chinese restaurant, and the next morning we cuddled in front of the TV. I fell asleep and Thimeo decided to go to the movies with my brother. They didn't want to wake me up and when I came out of sleep, I had the bad surprise to find myself alone, without Thimeo. While I waited for them to come home, I took the liberty of unplugging his game console, which I thought was very hot, which I found dangerous against the wood-paneled wall. When Thimeo came home he threw a tantrum, yelled at me for the console and locked himself in the kitchen... He asked my mom to go back to his uncle's house so he wouldn't stay with me. With Clément, we found this behavior unacceptable so we went back to the country that evening. Since then, Thimeo does not want to see me anymore. He will repeat his fourth year and go to a boarding school far from Paris, my parents not being able to have any authority over him. The objective is that he finds again the taste of learning with a regulated rhythm of life, without console or cell phone. I hope that this will succeed for him, I am very worried about his future.

I have become myself again, but I am not allowed to take my place as a mother. Camilla has never called me to ask about me, or to give me news of my son, or to send me pictures when she has him for the vacations. I tried to contact her to be together around Thimeo since we all want him to be well, but she refuses to talk to me. She buys my son by taking him to Corsica and giving him very expensive gifts...

My fight today is to find my place as a mother, as a woman who is still young with my forty years of age, to make Clément happy who has been completely devoted to me for three years. That my parents regain confidence in me, and thus by gestures, actions, that I can regain the love of my son, that he knows that I am once again THE pillar on which he can count again... I drowned in alcohol, I ask for his forgiveness, but my life was not easy and I did not know how to do otherwise. I hope he will forgive me, and that he will understand when he is older.

My heart is still sad but I know how to appreciate every minute that passes. If you only knew how good it feels to drink tall glasses of cool water, remember everything, not hurt anywhere, and truly be more alive than ever! It's a second birth.

I wrote this book to show how dangerous alcohol is, how easy it is to fall into it and how difficult it is to get out of it... I went through this path and it was extremely perilous, but the end of my alcoholism, I owe it to myself. Because I decided to. I want to tell you "YES, it is possible to get out of it! I did it!" Today I even ache when I see others drinking. I can gauge their level of addiction and the consequences in their lives. I have experience.

The subject is so vast, but here is my story, I hope to have turned the page on alcohol by giving myself to you like this. I would like to make myself useful, that my experience raises awareness, that my testimony gives hope and courage. There is always time to stop. Don't despair, even if there are difficulties of "after" - how to find your place with those you love and in society, how to find the confidence of your loved ones... The road will be difficult and long, I know it, I will have to be courageous. My son is my courage.

Drowned! I was drowned in alcohol. Today I am an alcohol survivor. Forever in my heart!

Afterword
By Dr. Fatma Bouvet
de la Maisonneuve[2],
Psychiatrist and Addictologist

As I spend more and more time with my patients suffering from alcoholic illness, I realize to what extent this disorder is a kind of condensation of women's problems and to what extent it is inseparable from the violence that women undergo today, whether physical or psychological, visible or insidious... Virginie Hamonnais testifies to this at every stage of the story.

Until recently, the issue of alcoholic disease in women was barely addressed, both theoretically and practically, although the damage is growing and specialists are alarmed.

The release of the latest OECD report in 2015, which shows a global decrease in alcohol consumption, but its increase in the youth and female population, marks a turning point. This report also shatters the received idea that a woman

---

2. Psychiatrist and addictologist at the Sainte-Anne Hospital in Paris, founding president of Addict'elles, essayist, author of *Les femmes face à l'alcool. Résister et s'en sortir* (Éditions Odile Jacob).

who suffers from alcoholic disease is a woman in a precarious situation: on the contrary, it is the most educated and those with the most professional responsibilities who are most exposed. The current concerns about violence against women must also attract more attention from professionals because the traumas they generate often lead to addictive behaviors. This is why doctors must always look for experiences of violence, denigration, disqualification, and toxic relationships, such as that experienced by the narrator with her son's father, who established a perverse relationship within the family. Despite a notable advance, the subject is still taboo, including within the medical world. Colleagues are still afraid of offending their patients by mentioning a problem whose pathological dimension they have obviously not yet understood. Some, as mentioned in this story, have little control over this misuse, which can be very serious, even fatal, and they go so far as to encourage them to change alcohol, thinking that stronger alcohol is more serious than weaker ones. "So, we went back to the addictologist with my mom and we talked about what alcoholism was and he explained that it could only come from me, that the physical withdrawal was real, and that even the medication was no match for the alcohol. My mother was trying to understand." Indeed it is difficult to understand.

Alcoholic disease in women evolves silently and becomes complicated more rapidly than in men. The figures we have confirm our practice and lead us to ask the authorities for a more significant investment in both research and prevention in order to protect women. They have become, along with young people, a major target for alcohol marketing.

Moreover, after having seen the packaging of vodka progressively feminized, we see today successful strategies to conquer the female market on alcohols that were once very male-sounding. The slogan of alcohol producers is "Women are the future of alcohol", just as young people are for unscrupulous salesmen.

To get an idea of the phenomenon, let's look at some figures. For a very long time, men's alcohol consumption was much higher than women's. However, the gap has narrowed considerably, especially among young adults. Researchers have reviewed 68 international studies on this subject. Among people born around 1900, men were 2 to 3.6 times more likely than women to drink. In contrast, among those born around 2000 and who are between 16 and 25 years old today, these ratios are only 1.1 times to 1.3, suggesting a near balance between the sexes (1). In France, between 2010 and 2014 the rate of regular drunkenness among women doubled while it remained stable among men. This would be due to an increase in female consumption, not a decrease in male consumption (2, 3).

The environment must also be taken into account, as working women suffer from greater ill-being at work (4). Overwork, mental workload and the link between working conditions and depression are subjects widely mentioned by our patients (5).

Today, women, along with young people, represent a very coveted market, as they are the ones who buy the majority of alcohol in supermarkets in France. Wine is still more consumed by men, but the gap is narrowing. Advertising campaigns are openly aimed at women: feminization of names and packaging, appearance of "light" wines, images featuring elegant and beautiful women: *Women have (become) the future of wine* (6). If awareness and prevention tools have succeeded in reducing the mortality rate linked to alcohol consumption by almost 40%, the obligation of prevention must be refined in order to protect women whose consumption continues to increase, with a rise in strong alcohol (7), as is the case for Virginie in this story.

The direct and indirect costs of alcoholic disease are higher for women because of the more serious complications that can occur with the first drink (8). Psychiatric complications - depression, anxiety and somatic disorders - but also liver damage, cardiovascular disorders or cancers. Mortality and morbidity are thus higher in women (9) which can be explained, among other things, by the effect of the product distributed on a lower total weight than in men (10).

If a woman drinks during her pregnancy, the embryo or fetus can be intoxicated by alcohol, which disrupts the development of the organs and results in fetal alcohol syndrome (FAS) or *alcoholic embryofetopathy* (11). In France, nearly 1% of births are affected, i.e. 7,000 new children each year.

Unfortunately for our narrator, as for many of our patients, many appointments are missed. Women represent only a quarter of the patients treated for alcoholism (9), even though they have easier access to general care. This lack of access is thought to be due to the shame and stigma that women feel in talking about an illness that still has a very negative connotation (13). The "Early Identification and Brief Intervention" (EIBI) program for alcohol, implemented by the General Health Directorate, makes it possible to circumvent this difficulty and to identify elements of alcoholic behavior in a few minutes in the most reluctant women concerned. Without a rapid diagnosis, they are excluded from the care circuits and their disease evolves. In fact, we have observed that women go first to specialists for complications (12) and that they are less likely than men to go directly to addiction clinics (13). When they do go, it is generally on their own initiative and with the idea of repairing the links that have deteriorated with their loved ones, most often their children. This family motivation improves the prognosis of the treatment. On the other hand, it should also be noted that if women consult specialized centers less, it is also because they fear the break with their children in case of hospitalization.

The pathway described by the narrator is unfortunately quite common as there are not enough adapted structures, whether they are emergency services or outpatient or inpatient care (cure and post-cure). It is usual that intoxicated patients are accompanied to the emergency room and are not considered as seriously ill, because the staff is taken by patients whose vital prognosis is at stake and is not sufficiently aware of the fact that it could be the same for all types of addictions, including alcohol addiction. This is why it is desirable to be able to welcome patients in other conditions, with a staff that is aware of the seriousness of addictions, whether in terms of withdrawal, abuse or psychiatric and somatic complications. Many addicted patients refuse the environment of a psychiatric hospital because they do not recognize themselves in the mentally ill people around them. It is true that the use of drugs introduces another dimension in the patient's condition and

Afterword By Dr. Fatma Bouvet de la Maisonneuve, psychiatrist and addictologist the way of dealing with it in a hospital setting. Nevertheless, my experience has shown me that there is very often a psychiatric disorder such as depression, anxiety disorder, post-traumatic stress disorder that accompanies the alcoholic disease, and that needs to be treated.

I am often asked if there is a difference in the relationship to alcohol between men and women. How do you recognize it? When to worry? The narrator gives us a fairly clear explanation by describing her father's drinking habits, which no one in the family emphasizes because it is "normal for a man to abuse from time to time. The alcoholic disease in women generally manifests itself in a context of loneliness, sadness and even depression. Drinking is often ritualized, for example every evening when they come home from work. When they are with their families, they drink in secret or they trivialize the situation and use the tension of the day as an excuse to have an aperitif with friends and family. They often describe their consumption as a dipsomania. The desired effect is a quick relaxation to "forget or knock themselves out". These behaviours generally correspond to moments of emotional conflict. The other clinical characteristic is a guilt of the following day. This guilt is almost systematically found in women who tend to disqualify themselves, even more so when it comes to this product that is loaded with moral judgments. This guilt is associated with the inability to abstain from drinking, as if they did not have enough willpower. This guilt also reminds them of their low self-esteem and the weight of other people's opinions.

The modalities of onset are changing. A few years ago, we described a late onset, around the age of forty; today it is much earlier and occurs, for example, in a school or festive professional context (in certain high-risk and highly feminized professions). Intense consumption in the form of *binge drinking*, this form of intensive one-off drinking sometimes followed by a blackout, is developing. Blackouts, to the point of forgetting how you got home, are more frequent among women (13, 14). They describe a *craving* (the irrepressible desire to consume) that is stronger than that of men, and is more intense when there is a comorbidity (15).

The triggers are emotional and relational, often disqualifying and humiliating. They are related to violence and occur in private life or in the workplace. The links are more and more frequent with a malaise at work. These women almost systematically describe low self-esteem, a recurring feeling of illegitimacy in their jobs and a strong preoccupation with performance, accompanied by guilt. This state of daily tension, visible violence or repeated and trivialized microtraumas can lead them to self-medicate by resorting to alcohol or other products (5). "I was not respected and loved as I wanted to be. Not as a wife, not as a mother. He paid almost no attention to his son, except to hug him on rare occasions, telling him he loved him. But love is not just something to be said, it has to be shown, lived and shared. It's too easy to say 'I love you' and walk away."

Not all women who are subjected to violence or who have experienced relationship difficulties become ill with alcohol. This pathology develops on a very specific terrain, described in the literature, but also verified clinically. Let's start with the personality. We often find in these women a "dependent personality" according to our jargon from the

DSM, an international classification of mental disorders. In this type of personality, there is a significant phobic dimension, low self-esteem with difficulty in asserting oneself, a lack of self-confidence and a difficulty in reacting to conflicts. I would like to make this clear here, because for a long time people spoke of hysterical personality which, in the psychiatric sense of the term, is not in principle pejorative, but which, being often attributed to women, has ended up becoming so. Thus, at the very beginning of the reflections on alcohol and women, it was quite easy to qualify them as hysterical in the sense of histrionics, of the affective quest and of the amplification of the events, that is to say of theatricalization. However, it turns out that this overly simplistic hypothesis has been disproved today. Paradoxically, these women simultaneously display a capacity to assume numerous responsibilities with an uncompromising concern for performance, in line with their socio-professional status which, let us remember, is often high. Many of my patients are "hyperwomen" (12), a neologism in which they readily identify themselves. They attribute their behaviour to an identity conflict, as they feel trapped between so-called feminine traits and the duty to function in the opposite way to their nature: *Be feminine and behave like a man!* (15).

As with men, family history is important to identify. When it is the first degree of inheritance, and even more so if it is the mother, this family factor increases the risk of alcoholic disease in women by 2 to 4 times (9). To a lesser degree, a family history of depression and anxiety disorders in female ancestors are also risk factors.

Numerous studies show that certain psychological disorders favour alcoholic illness in women, the first of which is depression (16). 65% of women (compared to 44% of men) suffering from an alcoholic disease have presented at least once in their life a depressive and/or anxious psychiatric disorder, compared to 36% of all women studied (9). Other work has emphasized the role of early anxiety or trauma such as bereavement or sexual abuse in childhood. If the trauma occurred before the age of thirteen, it is accompanied by alcohol abuse in proportions three times higher than those observed for the rest of the population. Virginia reported an incestuous past with her grandfather, which could very well represent a significant risk factor for the onset of alcoholic disease in her.

Some authors understand alcohol abuse as an outlet for old and deep suffering, but also as a form of expression of their experience as victims (9). These antecedents can be elements of poor prognosis or of resistance to treatment (17).

Marriage appears to be a poor prognostic factor for women, whereas it protects men from alcohol (15). This may be due to the occurrence of marital or family tensions as well as the accumulation of responsibilities. The story you just read illustrates this. The professional environment also has an influence on the behaviour of patients and in a way that deserves to be better analyzed, given the latest figures collected on alcohol consumption in the professional environment in France. On this occasion, the subject of women's job satisfaction and the sharing of domestic tasks should be addressed (4). Gender inequality in the workplace generates a lot of frustration and suffering that some women deal with by using products. And the more educated they are, the more likely they are to turn to alcohol.

The lengthening of women's lives is also an important risk. They are more exposed to the death of a spouse, which is a depressive factor. More of them live alone, which can push the most fragile of them towards alcohol abuse. This is how we can understand the progression of the disease at increasingly advanced ages (9).

Psychiatric co-morbidities, i.e. mental disorders, often accompany alcoholic disease and it is important to take them into account for more appropriate management. This is particularly true for women, for whom it is most often thymic (mood disorders, such as depression or bipolarity) and anxiety comorbidities, unlike men, for whom an antisocial personality is found (19). The association with alcoholism must be diagnosed to improve the prognosis.

The first of the comorbidities is addictive comorbidity (20). For women, these are primarily tobacco and drug dependence and eating disorders. In bulimics, for example, alcohol abuse is sixteen times higher than in non-bulimics (9). It is worth noting the current increase in the number of young women being consulted for alcoholorexia or drunkorexia. This phenomenon affects 16% of American students who prefer drinking to eating to calculate calories and to reach insensitivity more quickly (21). Depressive and anxiety disorders and early trauma are the next most common (9). Post-traumatic stress disorder is often found in the history of patients, particularly sexual violence, hence the importance of systematically looking for it (22).

In bipolar patients, the risk of developing alcohol misuse is greater for women than for men. It is often associated with other products (23, 24, 25).

On the borderline of comorbidities and complications is the issue of suicide attempts, which affect women significantly more than men. It is therefore important to bear in mind that this disease kills by various means and is by no means harmless.

The general principles of care are the same as for men. However, the clinical, individual and environmental specificities must be matched by an approach and listening skills adapted to women. Everything is usually done during the initial consultation, which is often the first opportunity to talk about one's suffering. Special attention, availability and empathy must be given on this occasion. Much of the therapeutic work is done when we explain to these women that they are ill when they thought they had a defect.

The neurobiological mechanism of reward has been clearly demonstrated for all addictions, so we have biological evidence of the disease, from which it emerges that nothing is stronger than what we depend on, in this case alcohol. Thus it is not a question of willpower, but of a psychobiological trap from which it is very difficult to get out without adapted support. The narrator says that she has never found a peaceful space to allow a fluid and supportive exchange, or that when she was there it was in a state of extreme severity. Caregivers are often very attentive and concerned about the patients' condition but it is true that their training on addictive disease and its severity is insufficient. We also know the overload of work that overwhelms them and we have to admit it here:

the taboo aspect of a woman affected by alcohol, including in the nursing profession, does not make things easier.

Care must be comprehensive: medical, psychological and social. It is important, if the patients request it, that the family is also informed about the disease. I have made it a rule never to share anything behind my patients' backs, even though the family often tries to get information because they think we are minimizing the amount of alcohol the patient has consumed. We are in a profession where we know that the patient may not tell us everything, despite the trust that has been established between us. If we want to maintain that trust, we cannot keep her out of the discussions that concern her. Families also need to know that it is not necessary to monitor the person who is drinking as this can have the opposite effect. Also, the highly intimate nature of the disease is not well known. Alcohol is a companion, as Clement reproaches Virginia, he is almost jealous of it. The state in which alcohol puts these women lifts the barriers and makes them plunge into the depths of their private life, both emotional, affective and sexual. They are in search of understanding themselves, of self-esteem, they reflect on their femininity, their desires, all subjects that they cannot share easily because they are either considered secondary to their disorder, or totally denied.

In addition, it is essential to keep in mind the legal and administrative complications that very often affect women. Withdrawal of license, indebtedness, dismissal, deprivation of childcare... These patients are subjected, in spite of their sick state, to the cookie-cutter judgments of sorcerers who claim to be psychologists and who, without seeing the immense suffering of the mother, allow themselves to accuse her of pathological and incestuous relationships with her children. How many of my patients are in this type of situation, trusting these people, some of whom ignore their distress and make them feel even more guilty? Here too we must emphasize the crying lack of training. Our association is more and more solicited so that these different intervening parties understand better this disorder, and particularly among women. They are right to want to be trained because this would place this question in the medical register and avoid moral judgments. Furthermore, women are the ones who manage the finances and sometimes they incur debts. In the case of separation, the question of child custody is to be noted as an aggravating factor, which sometimes leads to the worst.

Weight gain, which many people neglect in their treatment, aggravates their low self-esteem and is one of the first motivational factors to encourage them to seek treatment. It is important to be able to refer them to specialists.

When the situation requires hospitalization, time must be taken to explain the conditions in order to preserve the therapeutic alliance: the time spent away from home and away from their children is crucial. The process must be done with their consent, except in the most serious situations that justify hospitalization at the request of a third party, which was the case for Virginie.

It is obviously possible to get out of what some people describe as a "bunker", a prison in short. If the person is accompanied by an understanding and caring family, he or she is more likely to improve because dialogue is easier

Afterword By Dr. Fatma Bouvet de la Maisonneuve, psychiatrist and addictologist and trust can be reestablished that the family had lost. It is useless to monitor the person who is in the process of treatment, he or she will feel this weight and this can often lead to the opposite result, because let's not forget that one of the reasons for this consumption is the lack of self-confidence. So if the people close to them don't trust them, progress in care becomes more difficult. The goal is to learn to live without alcohol and for that you need to be accompanied, to have a space to talk about your thoughts, your emotions, your state, without this product. It is therefore necessary to be followed by a doctor until both consider that the patient is free of alcohol. Living without alcohol is difficult because it means changing your life and your rituals. I explain this to my patients so that they don't think the journey is always easy. Like Virginie, they tell me that they appreciate the simple things in life to the fullest, to rediscover the smells, to savor the food, to appreciate the colors, the nature. They feel more in touch with reality and, if it is not always simple, they have enough strength to face it without having to resort to alcohol to disguise the harshness of life. The subject of freedom and liberation is also about what a woman allows herself in her life in general. I often talk to them about an inner nugget to be found as the sessions progress. Many of them cry with emotion when I tell them about it, because it reveals the buried frustrations, the censures, the imposed ways that have pushed them towards alcohol to appease a desire that is too strong and that has been thwarted, or to have the artificial impression that it can be fulfilled thanks to the disinhibition that alcohol provides. One gets out of alcohol by expressing a creativity that has been censored and that will give a stronger sensation than that of drunkenness. This is what is exciting in the care of these patients, to see them transform from chrysalises to butterflies.

The seriousness of the effects of alcohol is no longer debatable, especially in women. It must attract the attention of professionals and public opinion because of the increase in its frequency and the serious complications it causes (26). The disease develops in vulnerable areas that must be systematically analyzed. Psychiatric co-morbidities must be investigated in order to set up the appropriate treatment. The alcoholic disease in women is still taboo and this is one of the reasons for their low rate of consultation in specialized services as well as for the long evolution of their disorder. It is through a global prevention work that we will succeed in reaching the target of women who are more and more affected by this disease. It is necessary to "encourage education, communication, training and awareness" (27) and to legislate on the promotion of alcohol in order to limit the appearance of disorders and their complications (4).

BIBLIOGRAPHY

1. BMJ Open journal, October 24, 2016 https://bmjopen.bmj.com/content/6/10/e011827

2. INPES2016 http://inpes.santepubliquefrance.fr/10000/themes/alcool/consommation-alcool-france.asp

3. Greenfield SF, *Women and alcohol use disorders*, Harv Rev Psychiatry. 2002 Mar-Apr, 10(2):76-85. Review. Erratum in: Harv Rev Psychiatry 2002 Jul-Aug;10(4):254.

4 Bouvet de la Maisonneuve F, *Le choix des femmes*, Paris, Éditions Odile Jacob, 2011.

5. http://www.oecd.org/fr/sante/l-ocde-expose-les-mesures-que-les-gouvernements-peuvent-prendre-pour-eviter-les-importants-surcouts-lies-a-une-consommation-nocive-d-alcool.htm 2015

6 Jean Aubry on the site le devoir.com, Sept 04.

7. 2003 Alcohol Observatory, INPES.

8. Lancet Health Journal, August 2018.

9 Limosin F, *Spécificités Cliniques et biologiques de l'alcoolisme de la femme*, L'encéphale, 2002.

10. https://www.ofdt.fr/publications/collections/periodiques/lettre-tendances/usages-de-drogues-

and-what-consequences-women-specific-trends-n-117-march-2017/

11. Academy of Medicine report addressing fetal alcoholization dated March 22, 2016.

Bouvet de la Maisonneuve F, *Les femmes face à l'alcool. Résister et s'en sortir*, Paris, Éditions Odile Jacob, 2010.

13. Schober R, Annis HM, *Barriers to help-seeking for change in drinking: a gender-focused review of the literature*, Addict Be-hav 1996;21:81-92.

14. Journal of sex 2017 https://www.tandfonline.com/doi/ref/10.1080/00224499.2016.1228797?scroll=top&

15. Wilson C., Otto S et al, *La femme moderne et l'alcool*, Liège, Pierre Mardaga, 1995

16. Liang W, Chikritzhs T, *Affective disorders, anxiety disorders and the risk of alcohol dependence and misuse*, Br J Psychiatry. 2011 Sep; 199 (3):219-24. Epub 2011 Jun 27.

17. Greenfield SF, *Women and alcohol use disorders,* Harv Rev Psychiatry. 2002 Mar-Apr; 10 (2):76-85. Review. Erratum in: Harv Rev Psychiatry 2002 Jul-Aug;10 (4):254.

18. INPES, *Substance Use in the Workplace*, January 2012.

19. Lyne JP, O'Donoghue B, Clancy M, O'Gara C, *Comorbid psychiatric diagnoses among individuals presenting to an addiction treatment program for alcohol dependence.* Subst Use Misuse. 2011; 46 (4):351-8.

20 Reynaud M, *Traité d'addictologie*, Flammarion Médecine Science, 2006.

21. University of Missouri-Columbia (2011, October 17). 'Drunkorexia:' A recipe for disaster.

22. Buckner JD, *Implications of comorbid alcohol dependence among individuals with social anxiety disorder.*

Depress Anxiety, 2008, 25 (12):1028-37. PubMed PMID: 18781667; PubMed Central PMCID: PMC2778209.

23. Nenadic-Sviglin K, Nedic G, Nikolac M, Kozaric-Kovacic D, Stipcevic T, Muck Seler D, Pivac N, *Suicide attempt, smoking, comorbid depression, and platelet serotonin in alcohol dependence,* Alcohol. 2011 May;45 (3) :209-16. doi:10.1016/j.alcohol.2010.11.004. Epub 2010 Dec 17.

24. Frye MA, *Gender differences in prevalence, risk, and clinical correlates of alcoholism comorbidity in bipolar disorder,* Am J Psychiatry. 2003 May, 160(5): 883-9.

25. Brousse G, Garay RP, Benyamina A, *Management of comorbid bipolar disorder and alcohol dependence,* Presse Med. 2008 Jul-Aug; 37 (7-8): 1132-7.

26 Lejoyeux M. *Abrégé d'addictologie,* Paris, Masson, 2009 (INSERM expertise).

27 Health and Consumer Protection Directorate General. Report: *Alcohol in Europe, a public health approach,* European Commission, 2006

TABLE OF CONTENTS

Table of contents

BEST SELLERS MAX MILO EDITIONS

Hitler's banker, Jean-François Bouchard

Confessions of a forger, Éric Piedoie Le Tiec

The Koran and the flesh, Ludovic-Mohamed Zahed

Governing by fake news, Jacques Baud

Governing by chaos, Collectif

A political history of food, Paul Ariès

Mad in U.S.A.: The ravages of the "American model",
Michel Desmurget

Mondial soccer club geopolitics, Kévin Veyssière

Putin: Game master?, Jacques Braud

Treatise on the three impostors: Moses, Jesus, Muhammad,
The Spirit of Spinoza

TV Lobotomy, Michel Desmurget